7

Digi Tech

Manasi Kashikar
Sneha Krishnan

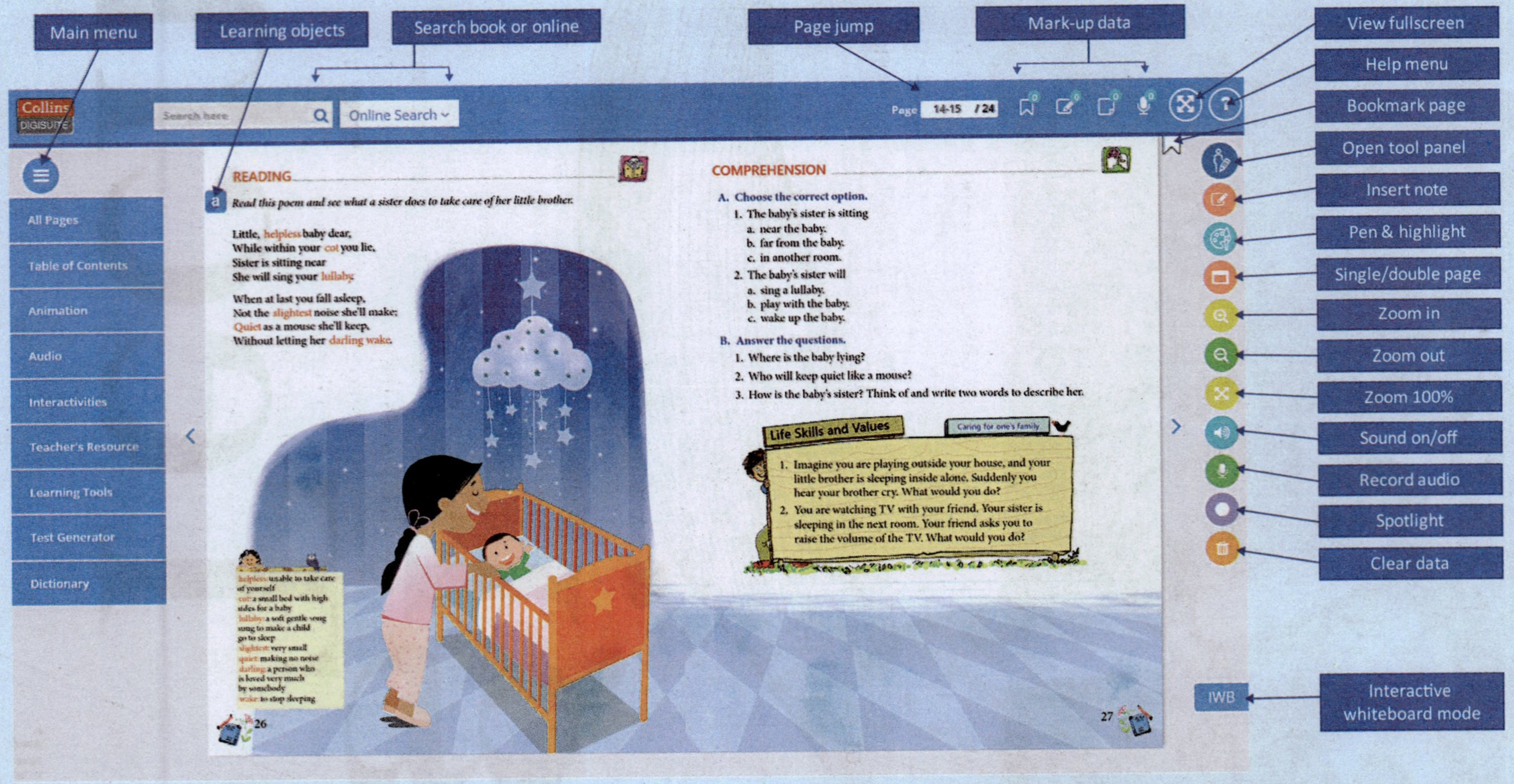

Student + Teacher

- **a** animations
- **ilt** instructor-led tutorials
- **ia** activities
- **w** worksheets
- audio
- **g** games
- **v** videos

Teacher-only

- **lp** lesson plans
- **w** worksheets
- **tn** teacher's notes
- **ak** answer keys

PREFACE

Over the last few decades, technology has touched almost all aspects of our lives. As technology continues to evolve more rapidly than ever, users are learning newer ways of harnessing the power of technology in their daily lives. In India, easy access to smartphones and affordable internet services have put the power of technology in the hands of millions.

In this backdrop, we believe, it is important for students to:

- ✓ Understand that technology is going to keep evolving. As citizens of the digital world that we all inhabit, keeping abreast of the latest advances is no longer optional, rather, it is an essential life skill.
- ✓ Appreciate that coding skills are as essential today as basic literacy and numeracy. This has been emphasized in the National Educational Policy of 2020 as well.
- ✓ Understand that technology is pervasive and they need to be able to comprehend its intersection with other disciplines. In other words, they need to learn to use technology as a tool to achieve a goal.
- ✓ Take control of regulating their usage and make constructive use of their access to computer devices.

While authoring this series, we have designed and presented the content with the intent of helping students in developing the skills described above. We have ensured that the topics are covered in a relatable manner and that the exercises are practical and applicable. The textbook along with its resources for teachers will enable them to deliver this subject effectively, while keeping the students engaged and interested.

In addition to the curriculum imperatives, we have included concepts as outlined in the National Education Policy 2020. Every grade has computational thinking–based practice problems that are aligned to Bloom's Taxonomy. Topics such as coding and app development have been given their due consideration as their relevance increases in the real world and while making career choices. Artificial intelligence has been woven into the chapters in an age-appropriate manner in the form of Fun with AI boxes, with the intent of enabling students to understand key concepts and applications of AI.

The series equips students with not only the skills required to excel in technology and make the most of it, but also exposes them to the practical applications of these in the world around them.

We would like to thank our intern Sejal Gupta in helping us shape the content.

KEY FEATURES

After reading this chapter, I will be able to:

- ✔ Recognize the components of a computer.
- ✔ Explain the usage of different components.
- ✔ Differentiate between external and internal hardware.
- ✔ Distinguish between external and internal hardware with examples.

Well-defined learning objectives that are mapped to the curriculum to help students identify the topics they will read about in the chapter

Activities and discussions based on real-life situations to set the context for what students are about to learn

Technology Literacy

Brainstorm and explore!

HTML is the markup language used to create websites. Write down the functions of each tag.

1. <i>
2. <sub>
3. <sup>

Soak up!

Pound signs (#######) in a cell mean that the column is not wide enough to display the cell content. Simply increase the column width to show the cell content.

Additional information/facts about the topic being taught

Contextual meaning of difficult words

Ganesh now stores all those records in a spreadsheet application on his computer. Just like books, a spreadsheet can store lots of data that can be updated regularly, is easy to store, does not occupy a lot of space, and will not get lost. Examples of a spreadsheet application include MS Excel, OpenOffice Calc and Google Spreadsheets.

In this chapter, we will be learning about MS Excel 2016 in detail.

spreadsheet application: a computer program with inbuilt features and tools designed to store and analyse large amounts of data

Technology Literacy

Crank up!

To AutoFit the width for several columns at the same time, simply select the columns to AutoFit and then select the AutoFit Column Width command from the Format drop-down menu on the Home tab. This method can also be used for Row height.

Tips and shortcut tricks for the topics covered in the chapter to foster inquiry- and discovery-based learning

Clear up!

Explore MS Access in the school computer lab and make a list of all functions of the Status bar and the Navigation toolbar.

Brush up!

If an 8-sided shape is called an octagon, what is a 10-sided shape called?

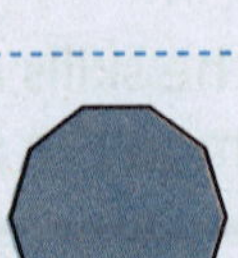

Hands-on tasks for revision, based on the application of the concept taught

Short questions to reinforce the concept learned and promote competency-based learning

Exemplifies the relevance and application of AI to the concept in the real world

Fun with AI

Inserting data with pictures is a new image recognition functionality introduced in MS Excel, which can automatically convert the picture to a fully editable table in a an worksheet, eliminating the need for you to manually enter the data.

Real-world examples and situations to help students establish linkages and connections to support the development of lateral thinking

Today I learned!

- Computer hardware is broadly categorized into internal and external hardware.
- CPU, motherboard, modem, SMPS, disk drive and ports are some examples of internal hardware.
- Input, output and external storage devices count as external hardware components.
- Input devices include keyboard, mouse and microphone. Output devices include monitor, speaker, and printer.
- A computer's memory can be classified into primary memory and secondary memory.
- RAM and ROM are types of primary memory.
- External storage devices such as SDD, USB Drive, CD, etc., are examples of secondary storage.

Link up!

MS Excel is used by most businesses today to track their accounts and finances.

Recapitulates all the important points covered in the chapter

Revision exercises comprising a blend of both objective and long-answer questions, including both fact- and application-based questions in a variety of formats

Revise and polish!

Learning Skills

1. Tick (✓) the correct answer.
   a. Which of the following parts cannot be seen till the CPU box is opened?
      (i) Monitor ☐ (ii) Software ☐
      (iii) External hardware ☐ (iv) Internal hardware ☐
   b. Which of these is not a part of CPU?
      (i) Arithmetic logic unit ☐ (ii) Control unit ☐
      (iii) Memory unit ☐ (iv) Application software ☐

Lab Activities

Experiential Learning

1. Open the antivirus software in your computer lab and answer the following questions.
   a. Which antivirus software do your school computers use?
   b. Run a quick scan to know whether the computer is infected with virus or not (avoid the full scan). How long does it take to run the scan?
   c. How many other scans are available in the antivirus software?
   d. Ask your teacher to show how to check for threats after the scan.
2. Create a presentation on different ways of preventing virus from entering the computer.

Based on the practical application of the concepts taught to enhance comprehension and provide opportunities for peer tutoring

Practical applications of the concepts covered to help analyse and understand real-world situations, with some extra effort put into research and information gathering

Projects

Find out about three endangered species of animals. Gather the following information about each:

1. What is their natural habitat? Where are they found?
2. What do they eat–herbivorous, carnivorous or omnivorous?
3. Search for pictures of male and female animals. Do they live in groups?
4. Why are they becoming extinct?
5. What can we do to prevent their extinction?

Use this information to put together a presentation. Format the presentation so that it looks bright and colourful.

Worksheet 1 (Chapters 1 and 2)

Critical Thinking | India Focus (IF)

1. Classify the following passwords as weak or strong.

a.	abc123	
b.	Qwerty9870	
c.	Summer29*	
d.	I-love-Rabbits&Cats	
e.	%fg34	
f.	bg12ok&**	
g.	football%	

Chapter-based revision worksheets focused on competency-based learning and one dedicated worksheet on developing computational thinking through playing games and problem-solving

NEP IN DIGI TECH

These are some of the key skills that you will see occurring throughout the books at various stages.

21st Century Skills

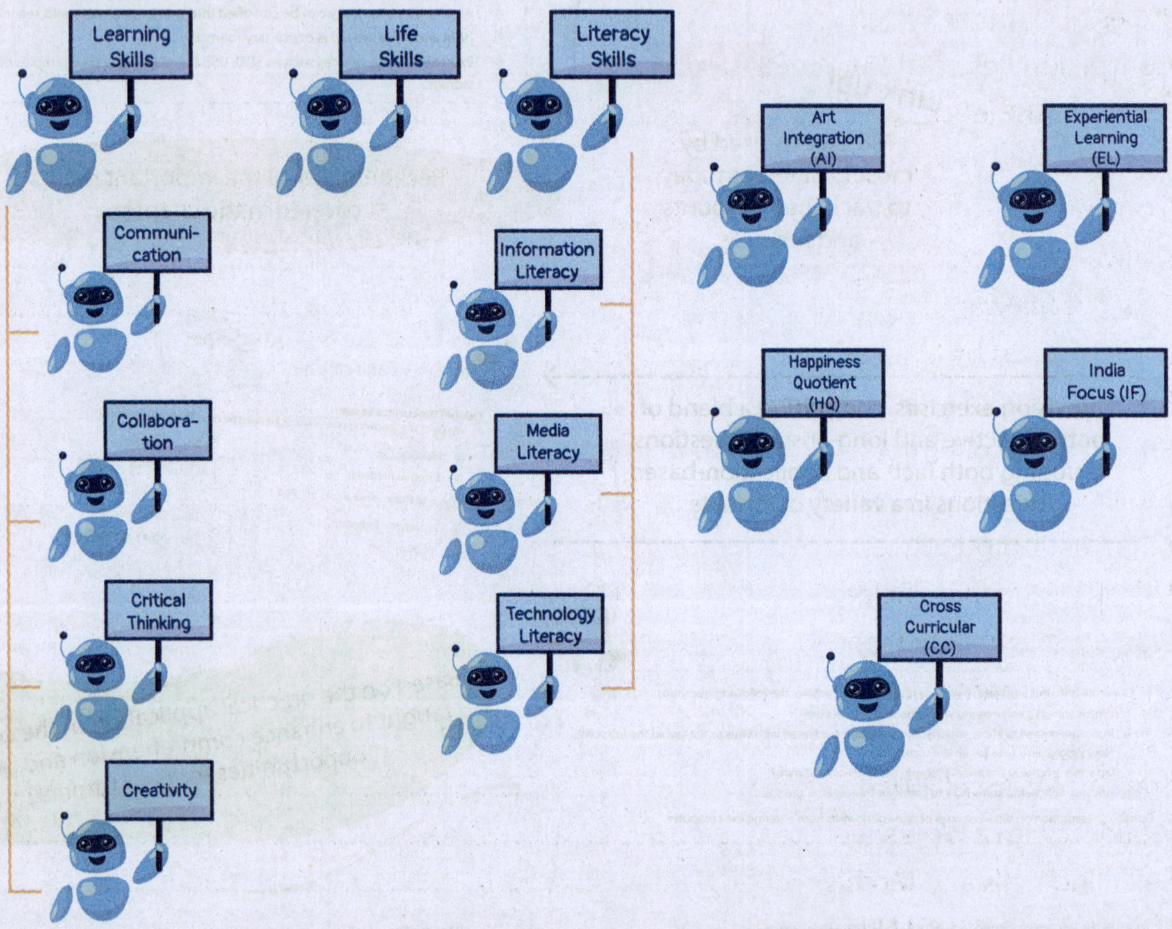

ABOUT THE AUTHORS

Sneha Krishnan and **Manasi Kashikar**, techies at heart, bond over their love of coding. They are co-founders of the company *MindChamp* where they teach coding to school students using fun, activity-based learning. They both love to teach students and that reflects in their work. Together with a team of educators, they have taught thousands of students to create computer games and websites. They want to make coding accessible to young students as well, so they are better equipped for the future.

CONTENTS

Chapter

1

Computer—Hardware Components

After reading this chapter, I will be able to:

- ✔ Recognize the components of a computer.
- ✔ Explain the usage of different components.
- ✔ Differentiate between external and internal hardware.
- ✔ Distinguish between external and internal hardware with examples.

Brainstorm and explore!

Technology Literacy

In groups of four, discuss the following questions:

1. Is a computer simply a box made up of physical parts?
2. Can a computer function if one or more of the physical parts are missing?
3. Do you know of any physical parts of a computer that perform a special function?
4. Have you ever seen anyone using a computer for a specific purpose only, such as creating artworks or designs, booking tickets or handling customer queries? How is their computer different from yours?

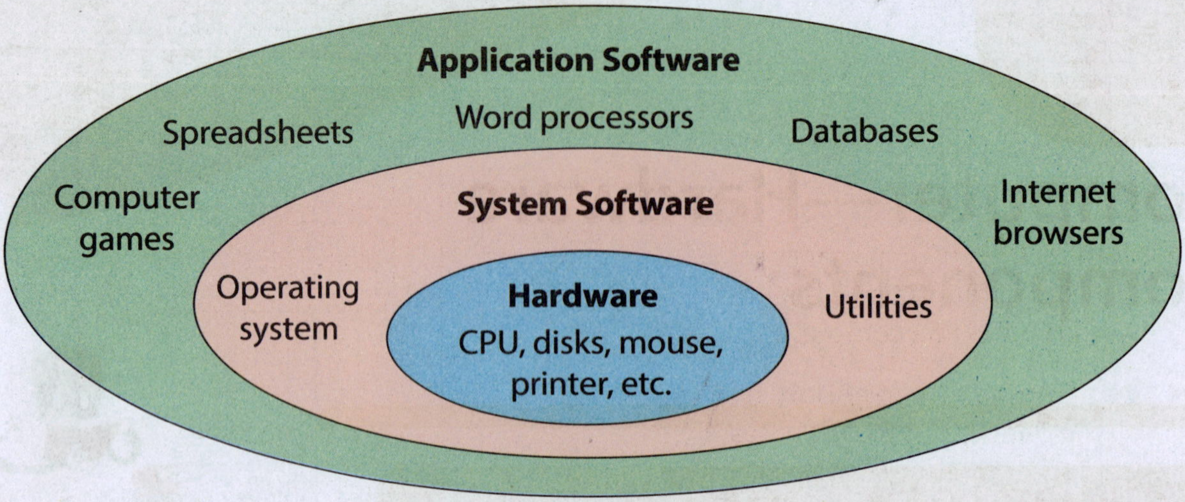

Fig. 1.1 | *Hardware and software*

Do you know what the statements given on the previous page actually mean? To understand that, we must know about the two major components of a computer—hardware and software (Fig. 1.1). In this chapter, we will learn about the hardware components of a computer. Hardware refers to those parts of a computer that we can touch and feel. Hardware is manufactured in factories and then loaded with software.

Components of Computer Hardware

Computer hardware is broadly categorized into internal and external hardware.

Internal Hardware

Internal hardware refers to the physical parts that are inside the computer. These parts can not be seen till we open the CPU box. Let us learn about the internal hardware components of a computer.

Central Processing Unit (CPU)

The central processing unit (CPU) receives the data and instructions from the input device, processes it and passes the result on to the output device. It also stores data (Figs. 1.2 and 1.3).

Fig. 1.2 | *CPU of a personal computer*

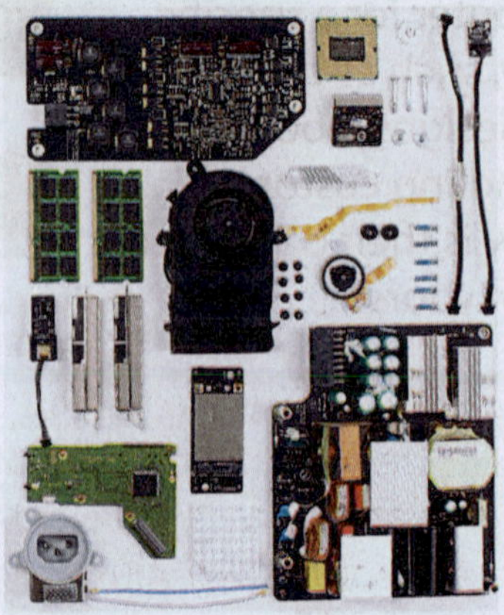

Fig. 1.3 | *CPU of a laptop*

The CPU consists of various parts (Fig. 1.4). Let us learn about them.

- **Arithmetic Logic Unit (ALU)**: It performs all the arithmetic calculations and compares numbers.
- **Control Unit (CU)**: It manages the flow of information between various parts of a computer.
- **Registers or Memory Unit**: It stores all the data that is to be processed. Computer memory can be classified as *primary memory* and *secondary memory*.

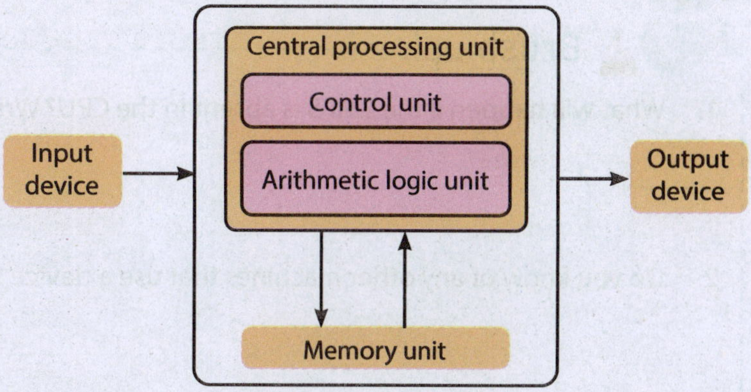

Fig. 1.4 | *Inside a CPU*

- **Primary memory or internal memory**: Primary memory holds the instructions on which a computer is currently working. It has limited capacity. Primary memory is of two types—random access memory (RAM) and read-only memory (ROM). We will learn more about RAM and ROM later in this chapter.
- **Secondary memory or external memory**: Data once stored in a secondary storage device does not get deleted unless the user does so. Examples of secondary memory include CD, DVD, USB drive and hard disk.

Motherboard

The motherboard is housed inside the CPU cabinet. It contains the components that handle the flow of information inside a computer. These include the memory, the ports that are used to connect to devices outside the computer, power supply, and so on (Fig. 1.5).

Fig. 1.5 | *Motherboard*

SMPS

SMPS stands for Switching Mode Power Supply. Electrical signals from a power source can be *alternating current* (AC) or *direct current* (DC). They can often vary in their intensity (voltage). The function of the SMPS is to convert AC or DC supply into an appropriate electric range DC acceptable by the computer (Fig. 1.6).

Fig. 1.6 | *SMPS*

Brush up!

1. What will happen if the SMPS is absent in the CPU? Write down your answer in the space below.

____

____

2. Do you know of any other machines that use a device similar to SMPS?

____

Disk Drive

A disk drive (Fig. 1.7) is a component that allows a computer to read from and write data onto a disk. The disk drive inside the CPU of the computer is also called a **hard disk** (or *hard disk drive* or *hard drive*). Application software are stored in the hard disk of a computer.

The other types of disk drives are *optical drives* (e.g., CD/DVD), *solid state drives* (SSD), and so on.

Fig. 1.7 | *Disk drive*

Modem

Modem stands for **modulator demodulator** (Fig. 1.8). It is a component that converts digital signals into analog signals. With the help of a modem, one can access the internet via cables or broadband. Modems can be classified into two types:

- **Internal modems**: Internal modems come pre-fitted in the CPU of a computer and are less than the size of a smartphone. Since they convert digital signals into analog and vice versa, their performance is measured in bits per second. An internal modem does not require a power supply other than the one used by the CPU. Dial-up connections via telephone and broadband connections are accessed via the internal modem.
- **External modems**: External modems are fitted to the computer with the help of a cable. They require a power source of their own.

Fig. 1.8 | *Modem*

Ports

Ports allow other devices to connect to the computer via a slot on the motherboard. In a conventional CPU, ports are present at the back of the CPU, whereas in a laptop, they may be on the side. The different types of ports that are commonly used are given in Table 1.1.

Table 1.1 | Commonly used ports in a computer system

Serial Port: A serial port allows exchange of data with an external device, one bit at a time. Serial ports are used to connect to modems, printers, scanners and so on.

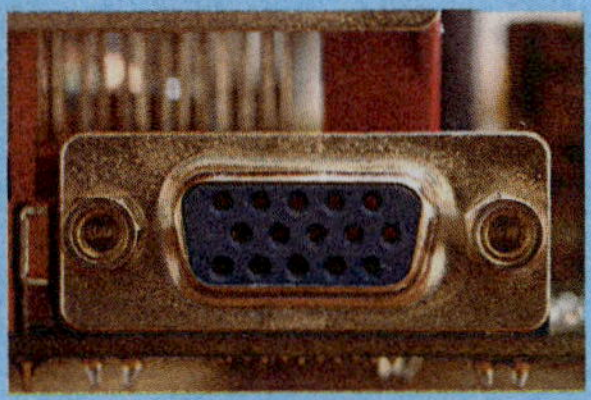

Parallel Port: A parallel port allows exchange of data with an external device, multiple bits at a time. Parallel ports are used to connect to external storage devices, printers and so on.

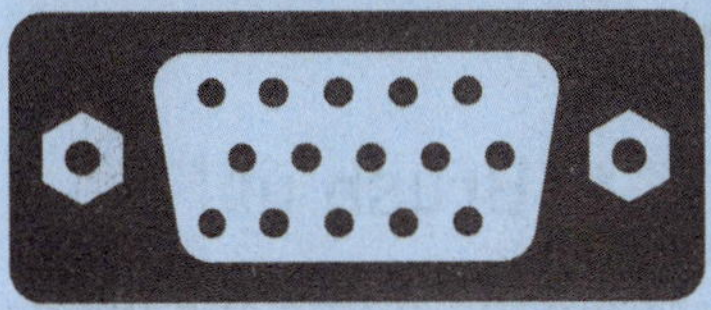

USB Port: USB stands for *Universal Serial Bus*. It is commonly used with a USB drive for storing data. USB ports are used to connect to a wide range of devices including printers, mouse, and smartphones via USB wires. It is indicated by the symbol ⭍.

HDMI Port: HDMI stands for *high-definition multimedia interface*. As the name suggests, HDMI ports are used to connect to multimedia devices such as HD monitors, projectors and gaming consoles.

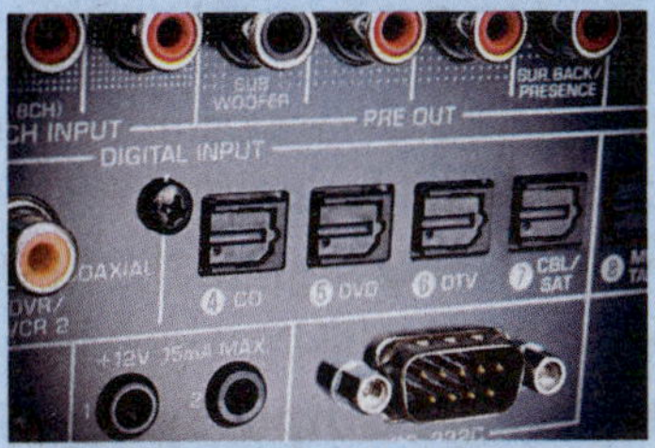

Ethernet Port: Ethernet ports are used for network connections either to local area network computers or to a wider network via the Internet.

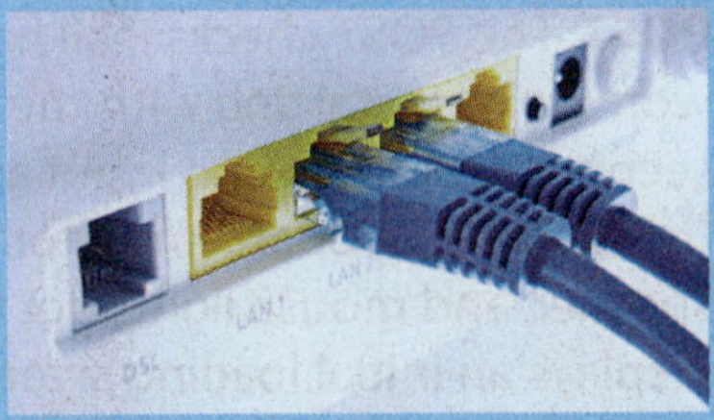

Sockets: Sockets are used to connect external audio devices to the computer.

- The **line in** socket is used to connect an external audio source to the computer. The **line out** socket is used to connect to speakers and headphones.
- The **Mic port** is used to connect a computer to an external microphone.

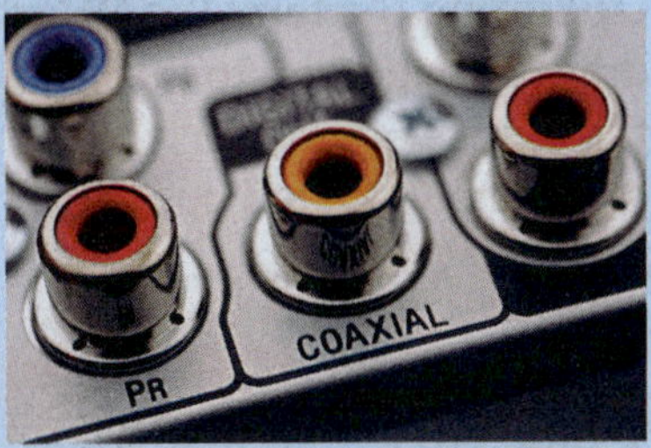

Apart from the ones we have discussed, other examples of ports include **power connector, PS/2 port, VGA ports, modem ports,** and so on.

Various ports and cables that can be connected to computers are shown in Fig. 1.9.

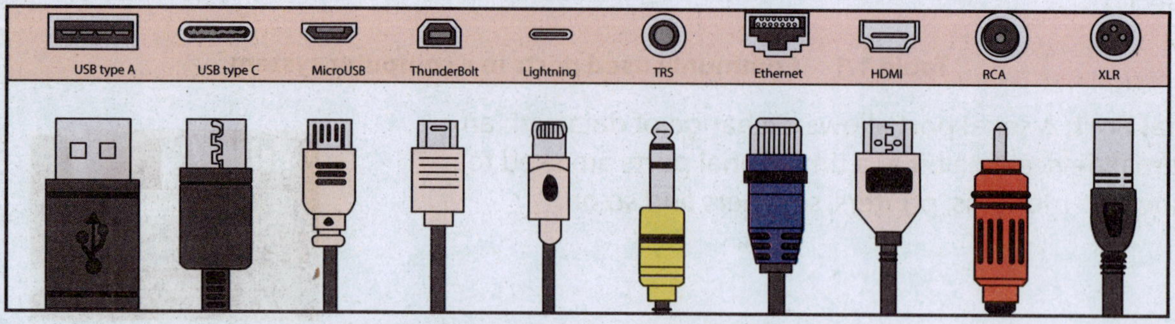

Fig. 1.9 | *Ports and their respective cables*

Brush up!

Apart from the laptop and the desktop computer, which other device(s) have USB ports?

____

Crank up!

Technology Literacy

The way all hardware components work together can be understood through the *Bootup process*—the process by which a computer is switched on. The following things happen when a computer boots:

1. **Power Good Signal**: The CPU gets power supply, which sends a signal to the motherboard. It activates the BIOS, which is on the motherboard.
2. **Basic Input Output System**: The firmware inside a computer that has the instructions for booting up is known as the BIOS or Basic Input Output System. The BIOS starts the power-on self-test (POST).
3. **POST**: The POST checks if all hardware components are working fine, starting with the RAM. It also checks for secondary storage and input and output devices such as the mouse, keyboard, monitor and speaker. The keyboard, speaker, and mouse lights get turned on, and the monitor displays an initial loading screen. When all the checks are done, the control is passed to the Operating System (OS).
4. **Operating System**: The OS, which is stored in the hard drive, is loaded on to the RAM by the BIOS. At this stage, the user sees the user login screen and the computer is completely booted up.

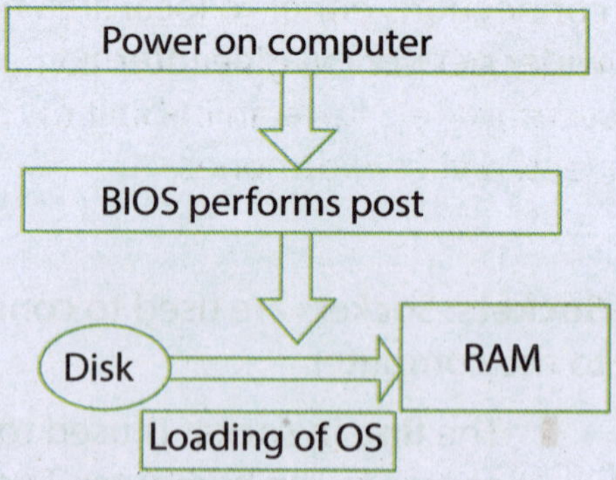

Link up!

The organization Raspberry Pi offers small, electric circuit boards that can be used to learn hardware programming the fun way!

External Hardware

External hardware refers to those devices that we can see and touch. Let us look at some commonly used external hardware.

Input Devices

Input devices are usually connected to the CPU through wires. Let us learn about some commonly used input devices.

Keyboard

A keyboard (Fig. 1.10) consists of several keys, which include letters, numbers, functions and navigation.

Fig. 1.10 | *Keyboard*

Soak up!

The most extensively used type of keyboard is called a QWERTY keyboard. The name denotes the first six letters on the keyboard. A typical QWERTY keyboard has 101 keys.

Mouse

A mouse (Fig 1.11) is used to manoeuvre across the screen. A mouse has right-click and left-click functions. A mouse can be connected to the computer with a wire or via Bluetooth. Mice can either be optical or mechanical. An optical mouse uses light to track movement. A mechanical mouse uses a ball to track movement.

Fig. 1.11 | *Mouse*

manoeuvre: move skilfully or carefully

Microphone

Sound inputs can be given to a computer using a microphone (Fig. 1.12). Most computers have an in-built microphone. Microphones can also be connected via headphones.

Fig. 1.12 | *Headphone with microphone*

Brush up!

Which part of the smartphone is used to give inputs? What is the technology called?

____

____

Soak up!

All laptops have a specified area that can be used to control the pointer on the screen, scroll through the pages, etc. This area is called the trackpad. It is equivalent to a mouse in a desktop computer.

High-quality Output Devices

Monitors, printers and speakers are commonly used output devices.

Monitors

It is hard to think of a computer without a monitor. Monitors are also known as **visual display units.** They come in various screen sizes and there are various technologies that are used to produce monitors. The different kinds of commonly used monitors discussed here.

- **CRT monitors**: CRT monitors were very popular till the early 2000s. CRT stands for **Cathode Ray Tube**. These monitors had a vacuum tube inside them that helped in the formation of pictures on the screen.
- **LCD monitors**: LCD stands for **Liquid Crystal Display**. They have liquid crystals inside them, which change colour when light falls on them. TFTs (thin film transistors) are a type of LCD Monitors. Unlike CRT monitors, which resemble a box and occupy a large space, LCD monitors are relatively thinner and lightweight. LCD monitors are widely used in school labs nowadays.
- **LED monitors**: LED stands for **Light-emitting Diodes**. They are made up of special materials that glow when light passes through them. LED monitors are also lightweight. Smart TVs, which are becoming increasingly popular, use LED technology.

Fig. 1.13 | *CRT monitor*

Fig. 1.14 | *LCD monitor*

Fig. 1.15 | *LED monitor*

Soak up!

With the advancement of technology, we have started getting better picture quality with higher resolution. Resolution is expressed in terms of width and height. The resolution of an image tells us about the pixel count and the size of the display. A pixel is the smallest unit of display on a screen. Simply put, pixels are the dots or blocks that are the building units of display on your screen. The higher the resolution, the more the number of pixels and the better the picture quality.

Brush up!

Using the internet, find out which technology is used in smartphone screens. Write your answer here.

____

____

Printers

A printer is a device that prints a document, image, or presentation on paper. Printers can be of different types, as discussed here.

Dot matrix printers: Dot matrix printers are one of the oldest types of printers. As the name suggests, the characters printed on the paper are made up of dots that are close to each other. The resolution of these printers is low.

Inkjet printers: Inkjet printers press the ink on the paper as a continuous stream. The resolution of inkjet printers is higher than that of dot-matrix printers. An inkjet printer uses ink cartridges to print both text documents and high-quality coloured pictures.

Laser printers: Laser printers are the most advanced and produce the highest quality output. They also print much faster than inkjet printers.

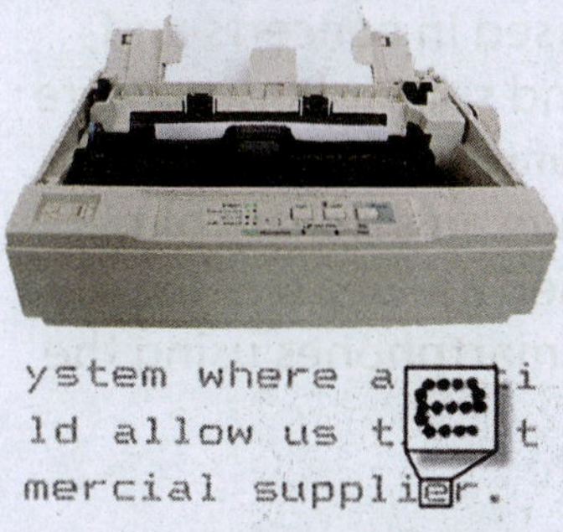

Fig. 1.16 | *Dot matrix printer and its output*

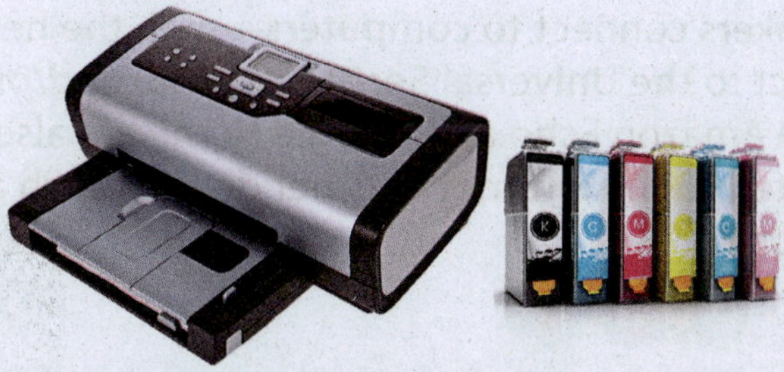

Fig. 1.17 | *Inkjet printer and ink cartridges*

Fig. 1.18 | *Laser printer*

Soak up!

Printers help us get the output of our work on paper. But did you know that printers can also be used to 'print' or 'make' physical objects. 3D printing is the process of creating a physical object from a digital model. To print any 3D object, we need to create a three-dimensional model of it using special designing software. Once the model is made, it needs to be sliced into different layers. The 3D printer prints one layer at a time. Hence, 3D printing is an additive process. An object is built up from 100s or 1000s of these layers. Layers are built up one after the other to create an object. Computer printers generally print a row at a time. The pattern is usually drawn with plastic, not ink. What makes the 3D printer three-dimensional is that once a pattern is drawn, the print head moves up and repeats the same pattern on top of the first. It is a bit like placing sheets of paper on top of each other to make a cube, but with plastic!

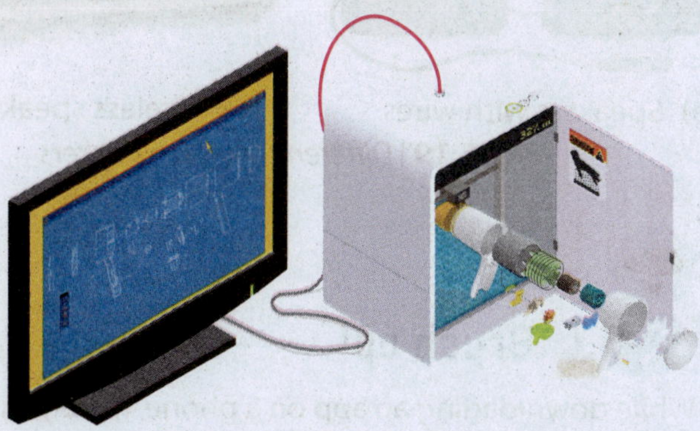

Technology Literacy

Crank up!

Plotter is an output device primarily used for printing. It is bigger in size than a printer and is used to make line drawings on paper with one or more automated pens. A plotter prints high-quality graphics such as charts, diagrams and maps and is used by engineers and architects. The different types of plotters are Drum plotter, Inkjet plotter and Flatbed plotter.

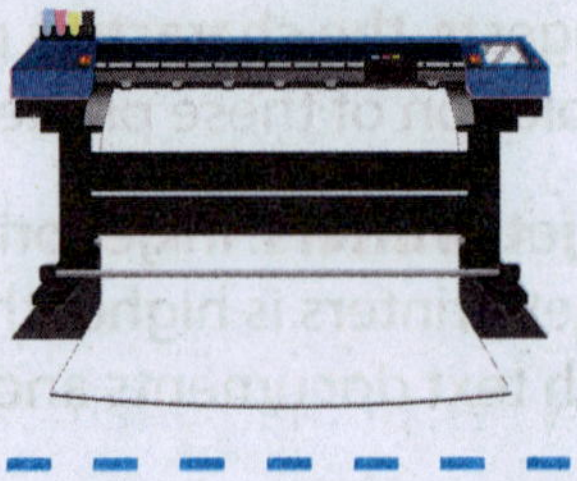

Speakers

Speakers are devices that produce an audio output. Speakers come in all shapes and sizes, right from the ones that can fit in the ear or palm of our hand to large ones used in concerts and stadiums. They can be connected to desktop computers, laptops, TVs and smartphones. There are two ways in which speakers connect to computers—with the help of wires and wirelessly. Speakers with wires connect to the Universal Serial Bus (USB) and/or have an auxiliary pin. Smart digital assistants like Amazon Echo and Google Home are also used as speakers to play audio. They can be connected to the internet or other devices such as smartphones using the Bluetooth or Wi-Fi technology.

(a) Speakers with wires (b) Wireless speaker

Fig. 1.19 | *Different types of speakers*

Fun with AI

Autonomous vehicles are vehicles that run without a driver. These vehicles extensively use robotics hardware and artificial intelligence.

Brush up!

While downloading an app on a phone, have you ever received an error message that says, "Storage Space Not Available"? Why do you think this happens?

Computer Memory

Computers can store several gigabytes of data today. In order to handle large amounts of data in a device, it is very important that:

A computer's memory is a physical device used to store data temporarily or permanently.

- it is stored effectively without getting unintentionally modified, damaged or deleted, and
- it is accessible quickly when required.

Various files and folders are stored in a computer's memory. A computer's memory is divided into two types: primary memory and secondary memory.

Primary Memory

Primary memory is accessed by the CPU. It is also called the internal memory or the main memory of a computer. RAM and ROM are two types of primary memory. Table 1.2 lists the differences between RAM and ROM.

Table 1.2 | *Differences between RAM and ROM*

Random Access Memory (RAM)	Read Only Memory (ROM)
RAM is used to store information temporarily when programs are in use.	ROM stores information permanently.
RAM gets erased when the computer is switched off.	It does not lose data when power is switched off.
Data stored in RAM can be modified and upgraded.	Data stored in ROM cannot be modified or overwritten.
It can store limited amount of data.	It can store very large amounts of data.
Accessing data from RAM is very quick.	Accessing data from ROM is comparatively slower.
The different types of RAM are: DRAM (dynamic random access memory) and SRAM (static random access memory).	The different types of ROM are: PROM (programmable read-only memory) that are produced as blank memory and EPROM (erasable programmable read-only memory).

Soak up!

Cache memory is a high-speed, quick-access memory that acts as a buffer between the RAM and the CPU. One of the most common examples of cache is in web browsers. If we visit a website frequently, the site information is stored in the cache memory. Thus, when next time we type in the URL, it loads very quickly.

Secondary Memory

The secondary memory of a computer refers to permanent storage devices. It is also known as auxiliary storage, external memory or flash memory. Secondary memory is non-volatile, meaning data does not get deleted even when the device is powered off. The data remains intact till it is deleted or overwritten. Examples of secondary memory include Compact Disc (CD), Hard Disk Drive (HDD), USB drive and Solid State Drives (SSDs).

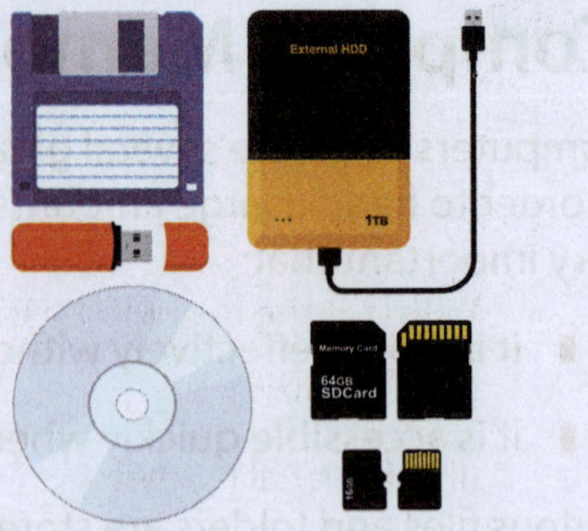

Fig. 1.20 | *Secondary storage devices*

Brush up!

1. Name the secondary storage devices you have seen or used.

   ....

   ....

2. Search the internet and list the storage capacity of a CD, a hard disk drive and a USB drive.

   ....

   ....

Soak up!

We have learned that read-only memory cannot be modified or updated by users. The instructions on the ROM are installed by the computer manufacturer. The permanent software placed on the ROM is known as firmware. BIOS is an example of firmware.

Today I learned!

- Computer hardware is broadly categorized into internal and external hardware.
- CPU, motherboard, modem, SMPS, disk drive and ports are some examples of internal hardware.
- Input, output and external storage devices count as external hardware components.
- Input devices include keyboard, mouse and microphone. Output devices include monitor, speaker, and printer.
- A computer's memory can be classified into primary memory and secondary memory.
- RAM and ROM are types of primary memory.
- External storage devices such as SDD, USB Drive, CD, etc., are examples of secondary storage.

Revise and polish!

Learning Skills

1. Tick (✓) the correct answer.

a. Which of the following parts cannot be seen till the CPU box is opened?

(i) Monitor ☐ (ii) Software ☐
(iii) External hardware ☐ (iv) Internal hardware ☐

b. Which of these is not a part of CPU?

(i) Arithmetic logic unit ☐ (ii) Control unit ☐
(iii) Memory unit ☐ (iv) Application software ☐

c. Application software are stored in the __________ of a computer.

(i) motherboard ☐ (ii) ports ☐
(iii) hard disk ☐ (iv) modem ☐

d. Which of these converts digital signals into analog signals?

(i) Pen drive ☐ (ii) Modem ☐ (iii) SMPS ☐ (iv) CPU ☐

e. Which of these devices has at least a serial port?

(i) Printers ☐ (ii) CD ☐
(iii) DVD ☐ (iv) Floppy disk ☐

f. What is the full form of HDMI?

(i) High-definition multimedia interface ☐ (ii) High-data multimedia interface ☐
(iii) High-definition multimedia internet ☐ (iv) High-definition media interface ☐

g. Which of these is not a type of port?

(i) Serial ☐ (ii) Parallel ☐ (iii) USB ☐ (iv) CRT ☐

h. Which of these statements is false?

(i) BIOS starts the power-on self-test. ☐
(ii) The BIOS in on the motherboard. ☐
(iii) The operating system is stored on the hard drive. ☐
(iv) When all the checks are done, the control is passed to the BIOS. ☐

i. Which of these printers is the most advanced?

(i) Inkjet printer ☐ (ii) Dot matrix printer ☐
(iii) Laser printer ☐ (iv) All of these ☐

j. Which of these is used to store data permanently?

(i) HDMI ☐ (ii) USB ☐ (iii) RAM ☐ (iv) ROM ☐

2. Fill in the blanks.

a. The ____________________ of a computer is used to do all the arithmetic calculations and to compare numbers.

b. The ____________________ memory is of two types—RAM and ROM.

c. The ____________________ memory of a computer refers to the permanent storage.

d. Sound inputs can be given to a computer using a ____________________.

e. SMPS converts AC or DC current to ____________________.

3. Write the full form of the following:

a. CPU ____________________ b. ALU ____________________

c. CU ____________________ d. BIOS ____________________

e. RAM ____________________ f. ROM ____________________

g. USB ____________________ h. Modem ____________________

i. LED ____________________ j. HDD ____________________

4. Categorize the following into internal and external hardware devices.

BIOS, ROM, Motherboard, Speaker, Monitor, SMPS,
Hard disk drive, Secondary, Pen drive, Modem

Internal	External

5. Categorize the following external hardware devices into input, output and storage devices.

Monitor, Scanner, Printer, USB drive, Speaker,
Projector screen, Microphone, Mouse

Input devices	Output devices	Storage devices

6. **Identify the following ports.**

a.  ____________________

b.  ____________________

c. 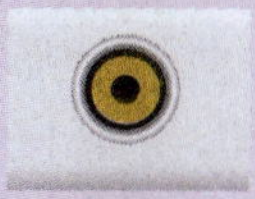 ____________________

d.  ____________________

7. **Answer the following questions.**

a. What is the role of BIOS in the bootup process?

b. Define ports in a computer system.

c. What are the main parts of a CPU?

d. Discuss the different types of printers.

e. Differentiate between the internal and external hardware devices. Give an example of both.

Think and Answer

Critical Thinking

Is Amazon Echo (Alexa) an input device or an output device? Discuss in the class and write down your observations with reasons to substantiate your answer.

____

____

Chapter 2

An Introduction to Number Systems

After reading this chapter, I will be able to:

- ✔ Describe the need of a number system.
- ✔ Describe the types of number systems.
- ✔ Convert binary to decimal number and vice versa.
- ✔ Understand the principles of binary arithmetic.
- ✔ Understand different bases of different number systems.

Brainstorm and explore!

Problem-solving

Sapan's sister Priya has challenged him to write the binary code for the following images. Help Sapan by writing the code. Follow the one that Priya has solved.

1. 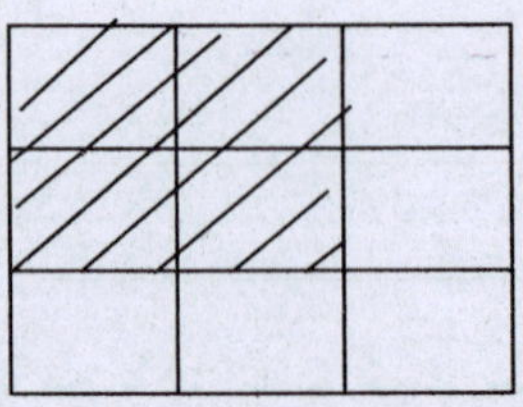

Binary code

1	1	0
1	1	0
0	0	0

2. 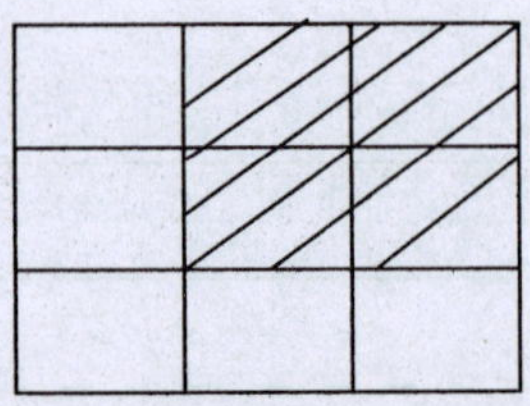

Binary code

3. 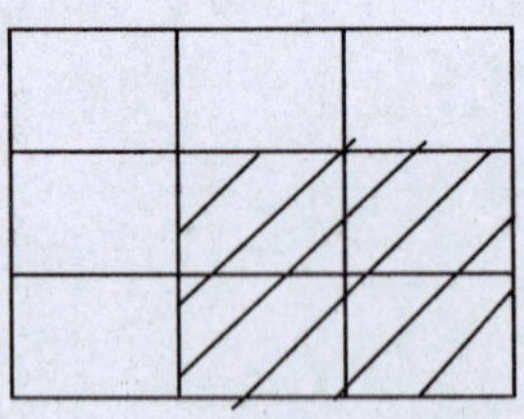

Binary code

4.

Binary code

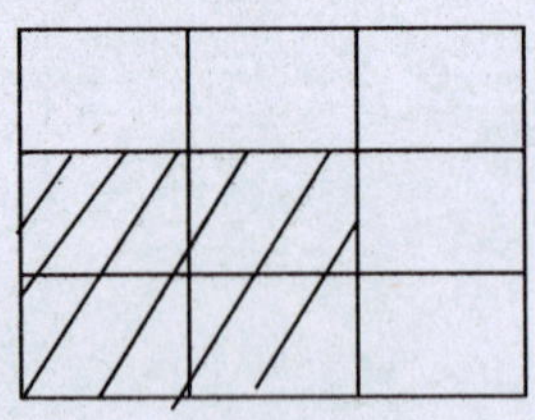

Humans usually interpret a question in their brain in the same language that they are going to respond in. Computers on the other hand, have a separate language of their own, which they process the information in. When asked any question, it translates that into this language, interpret or process that question and then re-translate before responding to the user. This secret language is called *Machine Language*. *Machine Language* consists of the numbers 0 and 1.

Number System

> Non-positional number system is one in which the value of a digit is independent of its position in the number. In other words, it is a non-weighted number system.

In our daily lives, we perform many tasks that require us to quantify objects or compare quantities, and so on. These days, we use numbers to count and quantify objects. Then, we make comparisons as per the principles of the system we used to count. However, this has not always been the case.

Although human beings started quantifying objects very early, people used fingers, sticks, stones, pebbles, etc. for counting in the past. From using standing lines or dots to knotted strings and pebbles, a variety of options was used to represent numbers. For example, IIIIII (six standing lines) or six knots would mean the number 6. Changing the position of any of the standing lines or knots would not change the value of the number. So, even when the second and fourth standing lines or knots are interchanged, the number does not change. Such a system is called **non-positional number system**. The Roman number system is an example of a non-positional number system.

Over time, we needed to be able to count ever-increasing numbers such as the population. Hence, **positional number systems** were introduced. In a positional number system, numbers are made up of symbols called digits (0, 1, 2, …9) that have a unique face value. The position of each digit in a number along with its face value is used to determine its place value. Thus, the digit 5 in 305 has the value 5 (face value = 5 and position in the ones column), while the value of 5 in 530 is 500 (face value = 5 and position in the hundreds column). Various positional number systems are decimal, binary, octal, and hexadecimal. You are already familiar with the decimal number system.

> A positional number system, also called weighted number system, is one in which every digit in a number is associated with a weight that is dependent on its position in the number.

> **Link up!**
>
> **The principles of number systems find many uses in a computer system such as creation of passwords, encryption of data, and so on. Did you know that the elevators in public places also rely on number systems for their smooth functioning?**

Types of Number Systems

Some popular number systems include decimal, binary, octal and hexadecimal number systems.

Decimal Number System

In our everyday life, we use the *decimal number system*. The decimal number system uses ten digits to represent numbers. These digits are 0, 1, 2, 3, 4, 5, 6, 7, 8 and 9. A combination of these ten digits is used to generate numbers. In this system, since there are ten different symbols or numerals, the base of decimal number system is 10. Consider the number 2345. It can be expanded as:

2	3	4	5	=	$2 \times 1000 + 3 \times 100 + 4 \times 10 + 5$
Thousand's place	Hundred's place	Ten's place	One's place		

This is written as 2345_d or $(2345)_{10}$ or simply 2345. This is read as two-three-four-five to the base 10. It is also a positional value system. This means that the value of digits will depend on their position and keep on increasing from right to left.

In the decimal number system, the digit on the extreme right has the least weightage and is thus called the least significant digit (LSD), whereas the one on the extreme left has the highest is the most significant bit (MSD) with most weightage.

A computer is an electronic device that receives instructions through electric signals. Having ten different voltages to implement a decimal number system in digital equipment is difficult. So, many number systems that are easier to implement digitally have been developed. Let us look at them in detail.

Fun with AI

BF16 (BFloat 16 or Brain Float 16) is a new number format developed for AI at Google Brain. Using BF16 helps to reduce the energy consumption and increase the computing power of systems performing AI calculations. BF16 uses 16-bit numbers to enable computers to perform calculations more rapidly without affecting the overall quality of the predictions. The chips required to perform calculations using BF16 are smaller than the chips that are currently used in desktop and laptop computers.

Binary Number System

The binary number system uses only two symbols or digits, 0 and 1. The word 'binary' is derived from 'bi' meaning 'two'. The binary number system is used in computers and electronics. Computers use 0 and 1 to represent all data and instructions. The rules of arithmetic in the binary number system are different from the common rules you are familiar with. In the binary number system, 1 represents the presence of the signal (ON) and 0 represents the absence of the signal (OFF). Thus, each digit of the binary number system is associated with a specific state. This helps to increase the speed of processing.

When we type any letter or word into a computer, the computer translates them into a series of 0s and 1s. All the data stored in a computer is stored in the form of 0s and 1s. Whether it is letters, digits, pictures, sounds, all of it is stored as 0s and 1s. Thus, 0s and 1s make up the binary system of counting.

In the binary system, each digit has a value expressed in powers of 2. Consider the binary number 11001, it is represented as shown in Table 2.1.

Table 2.1 *Binary number system*

Base 2	2^4 (MSB)	2^3	2^2	2^1	2^0 (LSB)
Value	1	1	0	0	1

Soak up!

Electric signals in a computer work as small gates that switch on or off. When it is off, the computer reads it as 0. When it is on, the computer reads it as 1. Though 0 is not actually no signal but signal at a lower voltage.

A binary number is made up of **bi**nary digi**ts** or in short, *bits*. For example, the binary equivalent of the decimal number 5 is 101, which is 3-bits long. Similarly, each digit of the decimal number system can be represented by a combination of 0s and 1s (binary numbers).

In any binary number, the rightmost digit is called least significant bit (LSB) and the leftmost digit is called most significant bit (MSB).

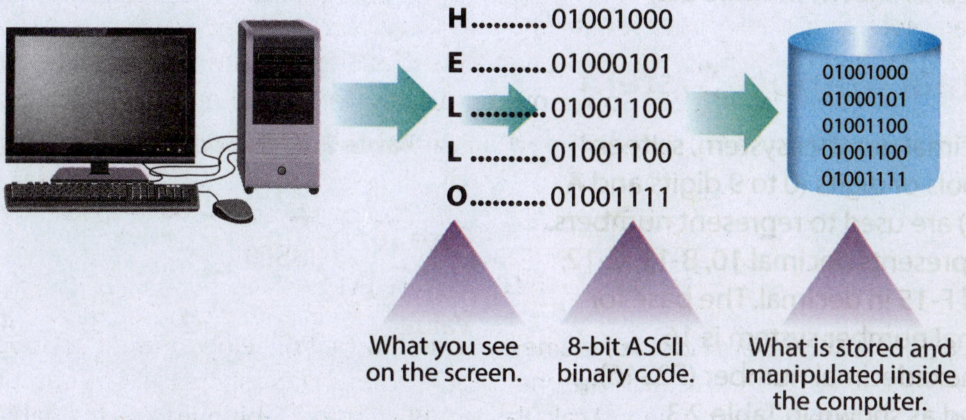

Fig. 2.1 | *How computers read user input using machine language*

All computers store data and perform all operations using binary numbers alone. All the numbers we type into a computer are converted to binary numbers before being processed and then re-translated to decimal numbers before output. In fact, a compiled software program is stored as binary code in the CPU (Fig. 2.1).

Clear up!

Find out if there is a server room in your school. Discuss with your teacher about the steps taken to keep it cool. Why do you think this is required?

Brush up!

If an 8-sided shape is called an octagon, what is a 10-sided shape called?

____

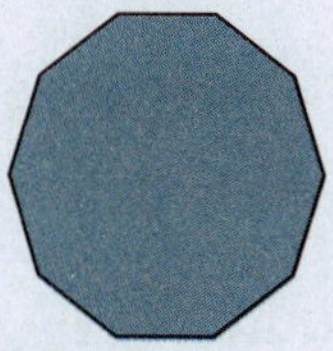

Soak up!

In number conversion systems, 'subscripts' or base numbers are used to indicate the relevant base numbering system, $1001_2 = 9_{10}$. Thus, 1001 is a binary number that is equivalent to the decimal number 9.

If no subscript is used after a number, then it is generally assumed to be decimal number.

Octal Number System

The octal number system has eight different digits: 0, 1, 2, 3, 4, 5, 6, and 7. So, the base of this number system is 8. Each digit is expressed as a power of 8. Consider the octal number $(52471)_8$, it is represented as shown in Table 2.2.

Table 2.2 *Octal number system*

Base 8	8^4 (MSD)	8^3	8^2	8^1	8^0 (LSD)
Value	5	2	4	7	1

Hexadecimal Number System

In the hexadecimal number system, sixteen different symbols or digits (0 to 9 digits and A to F alphabets) are used to represent numbers. The letter A represents decimal 10, B-11, C-12, D-13, E-14 and F-15 in decimal. The base for the hexadecimal number system is 16. Consider the hexadecimal number $(F2346)_{16}$, it is represented as shown in Table 2.3.

Table 2.3 *Hexadecimal number system*

Base 16	16^4 (MSD)	16^3	16^2	16^1	16^0 (LSD)
Value	F	2	3	4	6

Table 2.4 shows the decimal numbers from 1 to 15 along with their binary, hexadecimal and octal equivalents.

Table 2.4 | *The equivalents of the first fifteen numbers in all number systems*

Decimal	Hexadecimal	Octal	Binary
0	0	0	0
1	1	1	1
2	2	2	10
3	3	3	11
4	4	4	100
5	5	5	101
6	6	6	110
7	7	7	111
8	8	10	1000
9	9	11	1001
10	A	12	1010
11	B	13	1011
12	C	14	1100
13	D	15	1101
14	E	16	1110
15	F	17	1111

Conversion Between Number Systems

A number written using the decimal number system can be represented using other number systems as well. Let us see how this is done.

Conversion from Decimal to Binary

There are two commonly used methods to convert a given decimal number into its binary equivalent.

Method I: Repeated division by 2

To find the binary equivalent of a decimal number, follow these steps:

1. Divide the given decimal number by 2.
2. Get the remainder from step 1 as the right-most digit (least significant digit) of binary number.
3. Divide the quotient of the previous division by 2.
4. Record the remainder from step 3 as the next digit (to the left) of the binary number.
5. Repeat steps 3 and 4, obtaining remainders from right to left, until the quotient becomes zero.
6. The last remainder thus obtained will be the most significant digit (MSD) of the binary number.

To convert 44 into its binary equivalent:

	Quotient	Remainder
Step 1 : 44 ÷ 2	22	0 (LSD)
Step 2 : 22 ÷ 2	11	0
Step 3 : 11 ÷ 2	5	1
Step 4 : 5 ÷ 2	2	1
Step 5 : 2 ÷ 2	1	0
Step 6 : 1 ÷ 2	0	1 (MSD)

So, the binary equivalent of 44 is: $(101100)_2$.

Method II: Sum of the weights Method

Deconstruct the decimal number using the power of 2 and form the binary table (*see* Table 2.5). The first digit is the number 1 (2^0). The second digit has a weight of 2 (2^1), the third a weight of 4 (2^2) and so on.

Table 2.5 *Binary table*

Binary Base 2	2^5 (MSB)	2^4	2^3	2^2	2^1	2^0 (LSB)
Decimal Base 10	32	16	8	4	2	1

Follow these steps to find the binary equivalent of a decimal number using the sum of weights method:

1. Write up the binary table using powers of 2.
2. Using the binary table, identify the powers whose sum matches the given decimal number.
3. In the binary table, assign 1 to those powers of 2 that are used to arrive at the sum. Assign 0 to the remaining powers of 2.
4. The final result is obtained by starting from the MSB and moving to the LSB.

Table 2.6 shows the conversion of 44 to its binary equivalent.

Table 2.6 *Sum of weights method*

Base 2	2^5 (MSB)	2^4	2^3	2^2	2^1	2^0 (LSB)
Decimal	**32**	16	**8**	**4**	2	1
Binary of 44	1	0	1	1	0	0

44 = 32 + 8 + 4 thus we write 1 in place of 32, 8, 9, and 0 in the remaining powers of 2. Giving us the binary number 101100.

For example, the decimal number 20 can also be written as '16+4' (*see* row 2 in Tables 2.5 and 2.6). Whichever weights are used (*see* row 3 in Table 2.6), we need to write 1 in that position whereas, write 0 otherwise.

Conversion from Binary to Decimal

The decimal equivalent of a binary number can be calculated using two methods—the doubling method and the sum of weights method.

Method I: Doubling method

In order to convert a given binary number into its decimal equivalent using the doubling method, follow the steps given below:

1. Write down the binary number.
2. Starting from the left, double your previous total and add the current digit.
3. Double your current total and add the next left-most digit.
4. Continue doubling your current total and adding the next digit until you run out of digits.

To find the decimal equivalent of 1011001:

$(1011001)_2$

$0 \times 2 + 1 = 1$

$1 \times 2 + 0 = 2$

$2 \times 2 + 1 = 5$

$5 \times 2 + 1 = 11$

$11 \times 2 + 0 = 22$

$22 \times 2 + 0 = 44$

$44 \times 2 + 1 = 89$

Thus, the decimal equivalent of $(1011001)_2$ is $(89)_{10}$.

Method II: Using the binary table

To convert $(1011001)_2$ to its decimal equivalent, follow these steps:

1. Write down the binary table
2. Add the number 1011001 from right to left in row 2.
3. Highlight the numbers that are 1 and ignore the ones that are 0 in the decimal row.
4. Add the highlighted numbers.
5. Decimal equivalent of $(1011001)_2$ is $64 + 16 + 8 + 1 = 89$.

Table 2.7 shows the conversion of binary to decimal.

Table 2.7 | *Binary to decimal conversion*

Base 2	2^6 (MSB)	2^5	2^4	2^3	2^2	2^1	2^0 (LSB)
Binary of 1011001	**1**	0	**1**	**1**	0	0	**1**
Decimal equivalents	**64**	32	**16**	**8**	4	2	**1**

Soak up!

ASCII is the acronym for the American Standard Code for Information Interchange. It is a code for representing 128 English characters as numbers, with each letter assigned a number from 0 to 127. For example, the ASCII code for uppercase M is 77 and the lowercase m is 109. Most computers use ASCII codes to represent text.

Brush up!

Write the missing numbers in the binary table.

Base 2	2^0	2^1	2^2	2^3	2^4	_____	_____
Decimal	1	2	_____	8	16	32	_____
Binary	1	10	100	1000	_____	100000	_____

Binary Arithmetic

In binary arithmetic, basic number operations, such as addition, subtraction, multiplication and division are performed on binary numbers. We will learn to add and subtract two binary numbers here.

Binary Addition

In binary addition:

0 + 0 = 0

1 + 0 = 1

0 + 1 = 1

1 + 1 = 10 (termed as 0 carry 1)

Example: Let us add 111 and 011:

$$\begin{array}{r} 111 \\ +\ 011 \\ \hline 1010 \\ \hline \end{array}$$

To add more than two numbers, apply the same method by adding the first two numbers and then adding the next number to the subtotal.

Binary Subtraction

In binary subtraction:

0 – 0 = 0

1 – 0 = 1

1 – 1 = 0

0 – 1 =*1

*When we subtract 1 from 0 (in last point), number is borrowed (10 – 1 = 1).

Example: Let us subtract 1010 from 1111:

$$\begin{array}{r} 1111 \\ -\ 1010 \\ \hline 0101 \\ \hline \end{array}$$

Crank up!

You could convert binary numbers to their decimal equivalents, perform the number operations and convert the result back to binary.

Brush up!

Have you ever bought a laptop or a phone? Did you heard the salesman mentioning "8GB RAM" or "128GB storage capacity"? Can you tell what does this mean?

____

____

Storage Units in a Computer

Here are some commonly used storage units in a computer.

Bit: Smallest unit of data in a computer. A single 1 or a single 0 in a computer is called a 'bit'.

Nibble: A group of 4 bits

Byte: A group of 8 bits forms a byte, a unit of memory size.

KiloByte (KB or Kbyte): 1024 bytes (2^{10} bytes)

Word: A computer word is a group of fixed number of bits combined as a unit. A computer stores information in the form of computer words. The length of a computer word is called word-size or word length. It may be as small as 8 bits or may be as long as 96 bits. Computer word varies from computer to computer but is fixed for each computer. A computer with 16-bit word is slower than a computer with 64-bit word.

Link up!

As of February 2021, the largest hard drive on the market clocks in 18 terabytes of storage space. In 1990, a basic hard drive held about 40MB, with more expensive options able to store more than 100MB.

Technology Literacy

Crank up!

Unit	Description	Example
Bit	1 or 0	A single pixel in a black and white picture
Byte	8 bits	A single character
Kilobyte (KB)	1024 bytes	A small document is about 1–2 kilobytes
Megabyte (MB)	1024 kilobytes	MP3 files take up about 1 megabyte per minute
Gigabyte (GB)	1024 megabytes	1 gigabyte can hold about 300 MP3 songs. A computer has about 4GB RAM
Terabyte (TB)	1024 gigabytes	1 terabyte can hold about 100 DVD movies. Currently, we can buy up to 4TB hard drive

Brush up!

In computer terms, kilo means 1024, so 1 kilobyte is 1024 bytes.

However, it is not the same when kilo is used to measure a physical quantity as in kilometre (measure of distance) or kilogram (measure of weight). What is the value of kilo here? ________

Today I learned!

- A number system is a system representing numbers.
- The decimal number system is a base 10 number system comprising ten digits, that is, from 0 to 9.
- The binary number system is a numeric system that uses only 2 digits—0 and 1.
- Binary numbers 0 and 1 are made of single bits.
- Computers use only binary numbers to store information.
- The octal number system is a base 8 number system comprising 8 digits, that is, from 0 to 7.
- The hexadecimal number system is a base 16 number system comprising ten digits, that is, from 0 to 9 and 6 letters from A-F.
- A decimal number can be converted to a binary number by using the repeated division-by-2 method or the sum-of-weights method.
- A binary number can also be converted into a decimal number using the reverse method.
- A single 1 or a single 0 in a computer is called a bit.
- A group of 4 bits is called a nibble.
- A group of 8 bits forms a byte, unit of memory size.
- A computer stores information in the form of computer words. The length of a computer word is called word size or word length.

Revise and polish!

Learning Skills

1. Tick (✓) the correct answer.

a. Which of these is the binary equivalent of the decimal number 7?

(i) 111 ☐ (ii) 110 ☐ (iii) 001 ☐ (iv) 100 ☐

b. 1024 bytes make up ____________.

(i) 1 KB ☐ (ii) 100 KB ☐ (iii) 1GB ☐ (iv) 1TB ☐

c. The ______________ number system has base 8.

(i) Octal ☐ (ii) Binary ☐

(iii) Hexadecimal ☐ (iv) Decimal ☐

d. A decimal number can be converted to a binary number by using the following method:

(i) Sum of weights method ☐ (ii) Multiplication-by-2 method ☐

(iii) Division-by-2 method ☐ (iv) All of the above ☐

e. Which of the following is not a use of number systems?

(i) Perform mathematical operations, such as multiplication ☐

(ii) Drawing an animal ☐

(iii) Storing information ☐

(iv) All of the above ☐

f. Which of the following number systems has the smallest base?

(i) Decimal ☐ (ii) Binary ☐

(iii) Octal ☐ (iv) Hexadecimal ☐

g. Which of the following number system uses letters?

(i) Hexadecimal ☐ (ii) Binary ☐

(iii) Octal ☐ (iv) Decimal ☐

h. What is the decimal equivalent of $(1011)_2$?

(i) 11 ☐ (ii) 10 ☐ (iii) 20 ☐ (iv) 12 ☐

i. Which of these is not a binary number?

(i) 11111 ☐ (ii) 1001 ☐ (iii) 22222 ☐ (iv) 1011 ☐

j. What is the sum of 0 and 1 in binary addition?

(i) 0 ☐ (ii) 2 ☐ (iii) 10 ☐ (iv) 1 ☐

2. **Fill in the blanks.**

a. The full form of MSB is ____________.

b. A group of 4 bits is called a ____________.

c. The octal number system is base ____________ number system.

d. We can convert a decimal number to a binary number using the ____________ and ____________ methods.

e. The length of a computer word is called ____________.

3. **Match the following.**

a.	Bit	(i)	0 and 1
b.	Binary numbers	(ii)	Base-16
c.	Hexadecimal number system	(iii)	Binary digit
e.	Octal numbers	(v)	Base-10
f.	Decimal numbers	(vi)	Base-8

4. **State whether the following statements are true (T) or false (F).**

a. The octal number system consists of letters and digits. ☐

b. 101+10=11 ☐

c. Binary numbers are 0 and 2. ☐

d. MSB means the most significant bit. ☐

e. A kilobyte consists of 1024 megabytes. ☐

5. **Answer the following questions.**

a. What is the difference between positional and non-positional number systems?

b. How is the binary number system different from the decimal number system?

c. Write the first 10 binary numbers using the base-2 or binary table.

d. Explain the hexadecimal number system.

e. Why do we need number systems?

6. **Convert binary to decimal.**

a. 1001 b. 1111 c. 101

7. **Convert decimal to binary.**

a. 8 b. 15 c. 10

Chapter

3

Computer Virus

After reading this chapter, I will be able to:

- ✔ Understand different types of malware and explain how does it enter into our computers.
- ✔ Define a virus and list different types of viruses.
- ✔ Follow standard measures to prevent virus attacks.
- ✔ Identify symptoms of virus attack on a computer.
- ✔ Use a suitable antivirus software.

Life Skills

Brainstorm and explore!

Fill in the blanks using the given words.

steal money   light firecrackers   steal personal files   enter neighbouring houses

A thief enters a house in the middle of the night, undetected.

1. If this thief has entered with the intention of stealing, he will ________________.
2. If he has entered with the intention of harassing the owner of the house, he will ________________.
3. If he wants to steal more, he will ________________ as well.
4. But, if he has come into just prank the owner of the house, then he will ________________.

Either way, the house and the house owner are in danger.

Just as the actions of a thief harm the owner of a house, there are people who can become threats to computers and computer networks. Such people are called cybercriminals. They create different types of threats to a computer and infect. An infected computer can be made to perform one or more tasks to:

- make the computer behave abnormally;
- work very slowly; and/or
- lose important information.

These abnormalities in the behaviour of a computer system indicate that the computer is infected.

Malware

Malware is short for **mali**cious soft**ware**. It is designed to cause damage to a computer or network. As malware travels within the network, it infects the computer it moves into. Malware is capable of harming the computer without the user's knowledge.

Types of Malware

There are various types of malware. Some of these are discussed in detail here.

Virus

Virus is a form of malware that can self-replicate and spread from one host to another. It can enter into the computer as an attachment such as an image, audio, video, files or other downloads from the internet. Once it is entered in the computer, it can corrupt, modify or delete the data stored in it.

Fig. 3.1 | *Computer virus*

Types of Viruses

Computer viruses can be of many types, depending on how they work. Some of the prominent types of viruses are discussed here.

1. **File virus**: This type of virus infects the computer by attaching itself to an executable file. Once the infected file is opened, it spreads and infects other files on the computer. It can also infect files with .exe, .com, .sys file extensions. Examples include Sunday and Cascade.
2. **Boot sector/memory virus**: This infects the boot sector of the computer and is executed every time the computer boots. It is very difficult to remove/clean this virus. For example, the Parity Boot virus displays the message PARITY CHECK and freezes the operating system. Other examples of the boot sector virus are Disk Killer and Stoned.
3. **Macro virus**: This virus infects Word, Excel and other data files. It can also infect other data files around it. Melissa and W97M are examples of macro virus.
4. **Stealth virus**: It is a tricky virus as it changes the code that can be used to detect it. Hence, the detection of this virus becomes very difficult. The first stealth virus named Brain was spread internationally in mid-1980s.

5. **Multipartite virus**: It is a hybrid of the boot sector and the macro viruses. This type of virus is able to infect multiple parts of a system, including the boot sector, memory and files. It infects program files, and when the infected program is executed, it infects the boot sector. The first multipartite virus was the Ghostball virus and was discovered in 1989 by Fridrik Skulason.

6. **Polymorphic virus**: To avoid detection by an antivirus, a polymorphic virus changes itself each time it is installed. Some examples of polymorphic virus are URSNIF, VIRLOCK, VOBFUS and BAGLE.

7. **Source code virus**: It looks for source code and attaches itself to it in order to spread. An example of source code virus is Die Hard.

Clear up!

Do smartphones also get infected by viruses? Find out about the first virus that infected a smartphone.

Trojan Horse

A Trojan or Trojan horse is a type of malware that looks like a legal software to trick users. In reality, it is capable of opening a backdoor for a hacker or other malware to gain access to the computer information. Unlike viruses, Trojans are not self-replicating and are only spread to users who mistakenly download them, usually from an email attachment or by visiting an infected site. Slow internet connection is one of the signs that you have a Trojan in your computer. Some examples of Trojans are Exploit, Trojan-Banker and Trojan-Downloader.

Fig. 3.2 | *Trojan horse*

Fig. 3.3 | *Worms*

Worms

Like viruses, worms are capable of self-replication but can also spread automatically by sending messages to people on the contact list of the user. They can spread over computer networks by exploiting their OS vulnerabilities. Worms are very dangerous, and the most infamous examples of malware are Michelangelo and MSBlast.

Spyware

As the name suggests, this kind of malware silently spies on user activities. This can include our web browsing and login details, credit card numbers and other information stored on the computer. It is usually bundled with another legal/free software program and gets installed on the machine without your knowledge. Examples of spyware are Gator, Zlob and TIBS Dialer.

Fig. 3.4 | *Spyware*

Fig. 3.5 | *Adware*

Adware

Adware is the abbreviation of advertising supported software. It is a type of malware that opens advertisements while a program is running.

For example, ad pop-ups on websites or software programs. These are usually bundled with other software programs downloaded on the system. These are not very dangerous, but a few can slow down the PC due to heavy ad display, or they may show inappropriate ads. These are usually used by companies as a marketing tool. They could come bundled with another malware such as spyware.

Ransomware

This malware blocks a computer system or files and threatens to expose the data unless a ransom is paid for it. It encrypts the files and demands a sum of money from the user to decrypt it.

Like a worm, this can usually spread through phishing emails that contain malicious links or by browsing on an infected website, or through some other vulnerability in a network service. Ransomware creators usually target business-related data. Examples of ransomware are Locky, WannaCry and Petya.

Fig. 3.6 | *Ransomware*

Fig. 3.7 | *Rootkit*

Rootkit

A rootkit is a software program that can hide its presence and gain access to a computer without users' knowledge. It also bundles up with other software to enter a user's computer. Once installed, it is very difficult to find this virus.

Attackers can steal personal information, eavesdrop, download other malware, and edit or delete files on the computer. It can be detected using either rootkit scanners or by manually checking for any irregular activities done by the computer. Examples of rootkit are ZeroAccess and Flame.

eavesdrop: listening secretly to what others are saying

Soak up!

In 2005, Sony secretly bundled a rootkit with its extended copy protection software, which came with millions of CDs. The rootkit modified host operating systems and tried to prevent users from making copies of CDs. However, hackers were able to exploit the vulnerabilities in Sony's rootkit to gain malicious access to the affected systems.

Bot

Bots or internet robots can be used both in good or bad ways. Malicious bot is a self-propagating software that can automatically perform the tasks it was created for.

Bots can be used in botnets for stealing information from computers or networks or opening back doors for other malware or infected computers.

Considering some of them are also used for good purposes (such as chatbots used in multiple websites), it is difficult to differentiate between the good and the bad bots by using a basic antivirus software.

Fig. 3.8 | *An internet bot*

Fun with AI

In 2016, Microsoft released an AI-powered chatbot, Tay, to pose as a teenage girl and interact with people via Twitter. Within 16 hours of its release, the bot had posted 95,000 tweets. These tweets were hurtful and racist. Microsoft had to remove the chatbot immediately. This is one of the most popular fails of AI in recent times.

Soak up!

Botnet is a network of compromised computers or bots. The name comes from two terms 'robot' and 'network'. Spambots can send spam emails across a computer or network. Websites avoid this by adding CAPTCHA tests in their sign-in forms that can differentiate between the users as human or machines.

Sweeper

Sweeper is a fake antivirus program, also known as a **rogue**. Sweeper typically enters a computer system in one of two ways: either the computer user downloads Sweeper, thinking that it is a real antivirus program or Sweeper gets installed through a Trojan. It is a scam that will ask for money for removing or detecting fake virus in the system.

rogue: someone or something that behaves differently from others of its kind, often causing damage

Major Attacks by Malware

Some of the major attacks by malware have been discussed below:

- **Creeper** was the first ever virus detected on the APRANET in 1987. This virus displayed a message on the APRANET: "I'M THE CREEPER: CATCH ME IF U CAN".
- **The Concept virus** got accidentally shipped on a CD-ROM supplied by Microsoft in 1995. It was the first virus to infect Microsoft Word documents shared via email.
- **The Morris worm was released by** Robert Morris, a university student in 1998. This worm affected nearly 60,000 computers connected to the internet, slowing them down to a stop.

- **The Melissa virus**, written by David L. Smith, was the first successful mass-mailing macro virus. This virus targeted systems which were using programs, such as MS Word and Outlook. This virus created considerable network traffic and caused damage worth over $80 million. Smith was later sentenced to jail for this in March 1999.
- The **OSX/RSPlug Trojan** was the first malware for Apple Macs discovered in November 2007. The launch of this Trojan increased fears that Apple's platform may be targeted more by hackers in future.
- The **ILOVEYOU** worm created in 2001, spread about 45 million computers in just two days. Users received an email with an attached "love letter" that overwrote files with the extensions .jpeg, .doc and .mp3 on downloading. The malware then forwarded the malicious letter to 50 of the other user's email from the contacts. This worm caused damage of over $10 billion.
- The **SQL Slammer** worm took advantage of a bug in the code of MS SQL servers in 2003. It affected over 75,000 servers in just ten minutes, causing a damage of over $1.2 billion.

Identification of Infected Computers

Some viruses need to be executed before activation, while some are activated immediately on clicking or downloading. A user generally has no idea that a virus has been installed until their computer or other devices start behaving abnormally. An infected computer may have one or more of the following symptoms:

1. Slowing down of a computer: Once a virus enters a computer, it attaches itself to different files and overwrites data. It, thus, occupies a lot of computer memory that results in slowing down of the PC.

An antivirus is a software program used to prevent, detect, and remove malware from a computer.

2. Higher than normal internet consumption
3. Freezing or abnormal crashing of application software and/or the operating system
4. Modified or deleted files and folders
5. Appearance of strange files, programs, desktop icons, etc.
6. Multiple pop-up messages displayed on the computer screen
7. The homepage of your browser changed without your input
8. Inability to access the Control Panel
9. Your friends/family members receiving random messages from your computer/profile
10. Disabled security software

Fig. 3.9 | *An infected computer*

Ways to Prevent an Attack on a Computer

Malware needs a medium to enter into a computer system. These mediums can be either computer hardware or software or a web application. Let us discuss some of these in detail.

Fraud Emails

Some malware are attached as links or malicious attachments and sent via emails. Once the link or the attachment is opened, the malware enters the recipient's computer. It could also hijack the email id and send malicious emails to all their contacts. Before opening an email, always check these two important points:

1. Malware emails are usually easy to spot, as they have either a spelling or grammatical mistake. Avoid opening emails from any unreliable, suspicious source.
2. Do not download any attachment or click on any link sent by unknown sources.

Technology Literacy

Crank up!

"Congratulations! You have won a lottery of 5000$"!

Never open this email.

Bundled with Free Software

Many times, if we download a free software from the internet, it is usually bundled with other software. These could have a hidden malware in them. Similarly, downloading files from random websites could cause the same problem as downloading a software. To avoid this, keep these points in mind:

1. Download apps/software from reliable sources only.
2. Read the terms of the software you are downloading very carefully. Mostly, it is always possible to opt out of downloading the additional, free software bundle.

Infected Websites

A few websites can be malicious or hacked and can download a malware into the computer. To avoid opening such websites, keep the following points in mind:

1. Keep the firewall active to block suspicious websites.
2. Do not click on random pop-ups/ads that could take you to a malicious website.

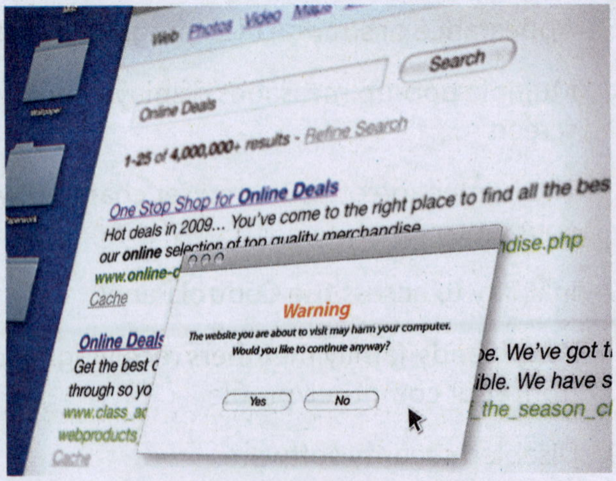

Fig. 3.10 | *An infected website*

Removable Drives

Malware can be automatically installed in a computer or network when an infected USB drive is connected to the computer. To prevent this, keep the following points in mind:

1. Disable the autorun function when you insert a pen drive or a hard drive.
2. Run a security scan on the drives.

Soak up!

Many websites use pop-ups that notify the user that their computer is infected (false alarm), and, in turn, provide a link to a website which could help them clean their machine (which in fact is the malware).

Apart from the malware mentioned above, many malware can also automatically download other malicious software. We can avoid these by installing the latest antivirus software.

Fun with AI

There is work in progress where AI systems are being trained to detect malware and detect even the minutest behaviors of malware or ransomware attacks before it enters the system.

Brush up!

Cross the odd one out:

1.
   a. Freezing of computer
   b. Random ad pop-ups
   c. Internet suddenly becoming slow after watching back to back movies on Netflix
   d. Sudden deletion of files

2.
   a. Downloading apps from Play store/Appstore
   b. Opening a forwarded email with random links from your classmate
   c. Keeping antivirus up-to-date
   d. Always keeping firewall on while accessing the internet

Effective Way of Protecting Computer Systems—Antivirus

Viruses can harm our computer systems and steal information.

Certain viruses are difficult to remove and the files can get permanently damaged. In such a case, these files are deleted by an antivirus.

An antivirus software, if installed on a computer, runs continuously in the background and keeps a check on every file and website that is opened, thus alerting the user of any virus, if detected.

Most commonly used antivirus software providers include Norton security, Kaspersky, McAfee and BitDefender. Microsoft Security Essentials is a free antivirus software that comes with all the Microsoft machines. AVG and Avast antivirus are some other free antivirus available easily.

How to Properly Use an Antivirus?

1. Keep the antivirus updated at all the times.
2. Periodically scan the entire system.
3. Run a quick scan of the system every now and then.
4. Check everyday if the scan is running.
5. Ensure the system/external device is ON throughout the time, the scan is running.
6. The antivirus software should be able to scan any downloads from the internet before they are downloaded on the system.

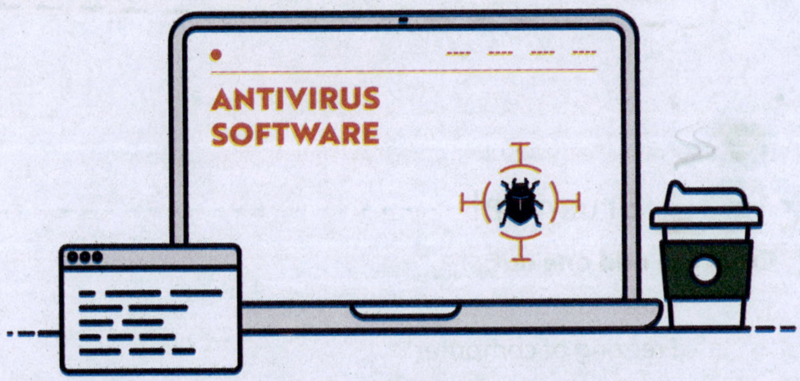

Fig. 3.11 | *Protecting a computer*

7. Follow prompts to remove potential threats.

Clear up!

Go home and see if all your laptops and computers have a firewall or antivirus software.

If yes, check if it is up-to-date or not.

Soak up!

Apple has included XProtect, Apple's proprietary antivirus software, on all Macs. This is inbuilt in the system.

Brush up!

Tick (✓) the correct answer.

1. Which of the following points should you take care of while downloading new software?
   - a. When in doubt, always ask a parent or a teacher. ☐
   - b. Check if it is a legitimate website you are downloading from. ☐
   - c. Uncheck any free random bundle of software. ☐
   - d. Antivirus is up-to-date. ☐
   - e. All of the above ☐
2. Which of the following symptoms indicate that a computer is infected with a worm?
   - a. A computer starts working faster than usual. ☐
   - b. The browser home page changes on its own. ☐
   - c. A random message is sent to your contacts. ☐
   - d. You suddenly require a code to access an image file. ☐
   - e. All of the above ☐
3. Which of the following is good for a computer system?
   - a. Virus ☐
   - b. Worm ☐
   - c. Trojan horse ☐
   - d. Antivirus ☐
   - e. All of the above ☐
4. Which of the following is a type of virus?
   - a. Macro virus ☐
   - b. Stealth virus ☐
   - c. Multipartite virus ☐
   - d. Polymorphic virus ☐
   - e. All of the above ☐

Crank up!

Windows Defender Firewall can help prevent hackers or malicious software from gaining access to your PC through the internet or a network. To open Windows Defender Firewall in Windows 10, type **defender** in the **Cortana bar**, and then click **Windows Defender** Firewall.

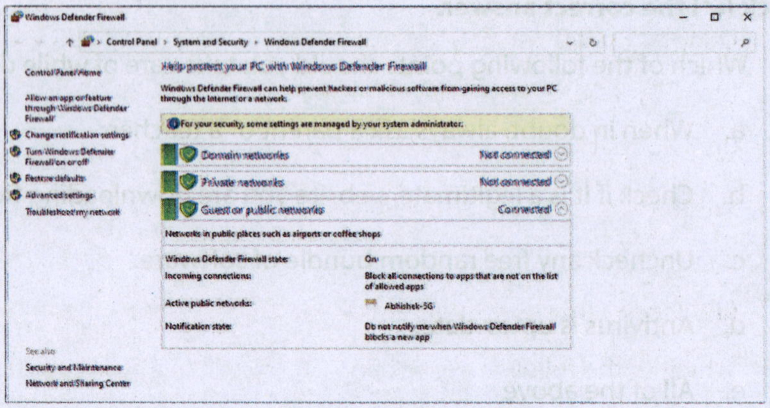

Today I learned!

- Malware is a software program designed to cause damage to a computer or network. It can enter a computer through infected links via spam mails, USB drives or infected websites and are bundled with free software.
- Virus is a form of malware that can self-replicate and spread to other files.
- Some of the different types of virus include file virus, boot sector virus, macro virus, multipartite virus, polymorphic virus, stealth virus and source code virus.
- A Trojan is a type of malware that can look like a legit software but is used to trick users by opening a backdoor for a hacker.
- Worms are like viruses but can also spread automatically to other computers connected to the infected computer by sending them messages.
- Spyware is a software program that can infect the machine and silently spy on the daily activity it performs.
- Adware is a type of malware that opens advertisements while a program is running.
- Ransomware blocks a computer system or files to expose the data unless a sum of money is paid for it.
- A rootkit is a software program that can hide its presence and gain access to a user's computer without the user's knowledge.
- A malicious bot is a self-propagating program that can infect its host and connect back to a central server called botnet.
- A sweeper is a fake antivirus program, also known as a rogue.
- Malware can be avoided by using an antivirus program or firewall and being vigilant while downloading anything from the internet.
- An antivirus is a software program that is used to prevent, detect and remove malware from the computer.
- Most common antivirus companies include Norton Security, Kaspersky, McAfee, Avast and BitDefender.

Revise and polish!

Learning Skills

1. Tick (✔) the correct answer.

a. Daily browsing and activity of a computer is monitored by ____________ malware.

(i) Spyware ☐ (ii) Adware ☐

(iii) Rootkit ☐ (iv) Trojan horse ☐

b. We should ____________ a link sent by a suspicious email id.

(i) open ☐ (ii) delete ☐

(iii) open and show to parents ☐ (iv) forward ☐

c. Which of the following is not an example of an antivirus software?

(i) Kaspersky ☐ (ii) Avast ☐ (iii) Spyware ☐ (iv) McAfee ☐

d. Which of the following is not malware?

(i) Virus ☐ (ii) Trojan ☐

(iii) Windows ☐ (iv) Trojan horse ☐

e. Which of the following viruses infects the Word, Excel and other data files?

(i) Macro ☐ (ii) Adware ☐ (iii) Trojan ☐ (iv) Spyware ☐

f. Which of the following is a type of virus?

(i) Memory virus ☐ (ii) File virus ☐

(iii) Boot sector virus ☐ (iv) All of these ☐

g. Which of the following is good for a computer system?

(i) Firewall ☐ (ii) Bot ☐ (iii) Worms ☐ (iv) Malware ☐

h. Tick (✔) the medium through which a virus can enter your computer.

(i) Download files sent by random people ☐

(ii) Making online purchases on Snapdeal or Flipkart ☐

(iii) Downloading software from Playstore/Appstore ☐

(iv) All of the above ☐

i. The ____________ affected 75000 users by taking advantage of a bug in the MS SQL server.

(i) SQL Slammer worm ☐ (ii) SQL Hammer worm ☐

(iii) Sledge Slammer worm ☐ (iv) SQL Slate worm ☐

j. Pick the odd one out.

(i) Malware ☐ (ii) Virus ☐

(iii) Trojan horse ☐ (iv) Worms ☐

2. **Fill in the blanks.**

a. ____________ virus attaches itself to the source code of the software.

b. Random ad pop-ups are caused by ____________ malware.

c. BitDefender is a type of ____________.

d. A ____________ looks like a legit software but is used to trick users by opening a backdoor for a hacker.

e. ____________ is a hybrid of the boot sector and the macro viruses.

3. **Match the following.**

a.	Avast	(i)	Trojan
b.	Bots	(ii)	Antivirus
c.	Malware	(iii)	Virus
d.	Stealth virus	(iv)	Internet robots
e.	Locky	(v)	Ransomware

4. **State whether the following statements are true (T) or false (F).**

a. Ransomware demands money to decrypt the target's file. ☐

b. Trojans are self-replicating. ☐

c. Worms can automatically send messages to all contacts. ☐

d. Bots pop up in a lot of advertisements. ☐

e. Spyware silently spies your computer. ☐

5. **Define the following terms.**

a. Ransomware
b. File virus
c. Adware
d. Worms
e. Antivirus

6. **Answer the following questions.**

a. How does malware enter into a computer?

b. Distinguish between a boot sector virus and a macro virus.

c. What are the different signs of an infected computer?

d. Discuss any two major virus attacks that have taken place in real life.

e. List the advantages of antivirus software.

Experiential Learning

Lab Activities

1. Open the antivirus software in your computer lab and answer the following questions.
    a. Which antivirus software do your school computers use?
    b. Run a quick scan to know whether the computer is infected with virus or not (avoid the full scan). How long does it take to run the scan?
    c. How many other scans are available in the antivirus software?
    d. Ask your teacher to show how to check for threats after the scan.
2. Create a presentation on different ways of preventing virus from entering the computer.

Collaboration

Group Activity

In groups of five, find out the different cases or examples of virus attacks that have happened in the world or from your personal experience. Create a presentation on it and show it to the class.

Critical thinking

Think and Answer

1. Priya loves to browse the internet. Many times, she uses hyperlinks to jump from one website to another. One day, she noticed that she started to get a lot of pop-up ads on her computer. Why do you think this happened?

    ____

    ____

    ____

2. Satvik received an email from chairman@sbi.com telling him to change his bank account details by clicking on the given link. Do you think he should go ahead?

    ____

    ____

    ____

3. While browsing, Ashwin found an update of his favourite game for free (which otherwise is 50 dollars) on one of the gaming websites. He was very excited but was not sure if he should download it. So, he asked his classmate Keerthana. Keerthana said she has downloaded from the same link and he should go for it. Do you think he should listen to Keerthana?

    ____

    ____

    ____

Chapter

4

Ethics and Safety Measures in Computing

After reading this chapter, I will be able to:

- ✔ Describe the importance of ethics in computing.
- ✔ Describe the advantages and disadvantages of using the internet.
- ✔ Describe prevalent unethical practices on the internet.
- ✔ Demonstrate how to stay safe while using the internet.
- ✔ Explain the meaning of digital footprints.

Life Skills

Brainstorm and explore!

As citizens of our country and cities, we use public spaces and share them with others. We follow unsaid rules to ensure peace and harmony. Mark the practices of good citizens from the following images. One has been done for you.

	**Spitting on the road** No, a good citizen does not spit on the road.
	**Not throwing garbage in the dustbin** _______________
	**Following traffic rules** _______________
	**Helping senior citizens** _______________

Just as we learn to distinguish between good and bad behaviour in our daily lives, it is important for us to understand the correct way of sharing information, communicating with other people, etc. while using the internet. In this chapter, we will look at some of these aspects.

Ethics in Computing

Laws exist to protect citizens and maintain peace and order. For example, following traffic rules prevents riders from meeting with accidents, thus making it safe for themselves and others who use public roads.

Computers and, by extension, the internet have become an important part of our lives. Any one with a smart phone uses the internet for the most basic things—talking to others, booking a cab, and so on. Just as we are citizens of India, we are also citizens on the internet. After all, from social media to online games, we all have virtual lives!

Fig. 4.1 | *Netizens*

A person who uses the internet regularly is called a netizen or citizen of the internet. Ethics in computing refers to the set of moral behaviour that serves as the guiding principle in the usage of computers and the internet.

While it is simpler than even before to access a variety of services over the internet, the increased usage of the internet has also put the users at risk in newer ways. Thus, it is more important than ever that we use the internet cautiously and follow ethical practices. Before learning the good practices to avoid these dangers, let us understand what we are trying to protect ourselves from.

Soak up!

Cyber law or IT law encompasses the legal practices that deal with information technology, software ownership, the transmission of information across the internet, user privacy and so on.

Unethical Practices Related to the Internet

The internet is a vast mine of information. This information can be both used and misused easily. Deliberate misuse use of information for illegal purposes, personal gain, etc. comprises unethical behaviour. Let us look at some of the common unethical practices on the internet.

Hacking

Hacking is the process of gaining unauthorized access to a computer system or an account. A person who engages in hacking is known as a security hacker or a black hat. A hacker, while remaining anonymous, tries to exploit the flaws in a system to gain wrongful access to private information. Hacking is a punishable offence by law.

Soak up!

Some of the largest companies in the world employ hackers to try and break into their security systems. This helps the company identify and fix any weak links in their security systems. The hackers who work for such companies are called White Hat hackers. They are ethical hackers who work to identify any weak spots in hardware, software or networks.

Fig. 4.2 | *Hacking into computer systems*

Plagiarism

Consider this situation. Your English teacher has asked you to write an essay on your favourite cartoon character. You think about the topic, list all the reasons why you like a specific cartoon character, and connect to the internet to get more facts about it. Finally, after a lot of research, you put together the essay for your assignment. Before submitting it to your teacher, you show it to a friend for their opinion. Your friend takes it to read and hands it over to the teacher as their assignment. Is this correct?

In this scenario, you wrote the essay. It is your copyright or intellectual property. Your friend used it without your permission. They used your content and claimed it as their own without giving credit to you. This is called **plagiarism**.

Plagiarism refers to the use of content from another person (or source) without their permission and claiming it as your own. Here, 'content' refers to any work such as artwork, photographs, music, films, computer programs, books, poems, blog posts, movies, plays, etc. created independently by a person or a group of people. Simply put, it is copying without permission. The internet is a great tool to create content and distribute it free of cost using social media and other websites. While using content from other content creators or websites, it is important to credit them as the owners of the content. Failure to do so may have serious consequences. It is a good practice to check the copyright details (often covered in the section Terms of Use) on a website/social media post and give due credit. Remember that any content that is free to use does not mean that it is copyright free. Spreading false information on the web is called fake news.

Fig. 4.3 | *Fake news*

Link up!

In India, the copyright of content creators is protected by the Indian Copyright Act, 1957. It not only holds up the rights of the copyright owners but also defines the meaning of copyright infringement, fair use, etc.

Fraud and Impersonation

When we use the internet to pay our bills, access our bank accounts, make purchases, etc., we provide a lot of important information about ourselves, including sensitive information that helps us establish our identity. For example, we need to provide the details of our Aadhaar card as proof of identity on many websites. Similarly, we tend to share personal details about ourselves on social media as well. If another person gets access to all of this information about us, they could use it to create a fake profile, conduct illegal activities like hacking, using our identity and so on. This is called impersonation. Such individuals tend to misuse the personal information of others for their personal gains. One's identity can also be misused to rob money online or perform illegal transactions.

Fig. 4.4 | *Impersonation*

Cyberbullying and Spamming

Cyberbullying refers to the act of threatening or embarrassing someone on social media platforms or over email. Bullies use the curtain of the internet to prey on others. It is a good practice **not** to talk to strangers on social media platforms. Interacting with unknown people, sharing private information like pictures, and sensitive information like passwords to various online services increase the risk of cyberbullying and theft.

Fig. 4.5 | *Cyberbullying*

Spamming refers to bombardment of unwanted information on users. As a matter of fact, when you log into your mail account, you will see a separate folder for Spam and Junk emails. Spam is nothing but unsolicited promotional material sent to hundreds of users.

Phishing

Phishing refers to the practice of sending fraudulent communications that appear to come from a reputable source. It is usually done through email. The goal is to steal sensitive data like credit card and login information. If you receive any communication that appears suspicious, check for small errors in the link. The link will lead you to a fake page that can includes spelling mistakes or changes to domain names. Never click on such links.

Soak up!

Smishing is an attack that uses text messaging (SMS) to execute the attack. A common example of a smishing attack is an SMS message that looks like it came from your bank. It tells you your account has been compromised and that you need to respond immediately by clicking on a link or calling a number. The attacker asks you to verify your bank account number and other details. Once they get the information, they can access the bank account and steal money.

Staying Safe in Cyberspace

While the threats may seem alarming, there are proactive steps one can take to stay safe. Let us explore how simple practices can go a long way in ensuring pleasant online experiences. The following are some common online activities and respective measures to stay safe.

1. **Install a Firewall/antivirus**: Cybersafety starts even before we connect to the internet. A virus is nothing but a program that replicates itself and starts inserting unwanted code in a computer. A firewall is a software (firmware) on a computer that prevents unauthorized access to the computer network or from it, based on security settings. Installing a good antivirus software on a personal computer, laptop and smartphone ensures any virus that makes its way to the system is taken care of. It scans for viruses and prevents it from affecting computers. McAfee, Norton and Avast are some of the popular antivirus brands. Windows OS has a built-in firewall.

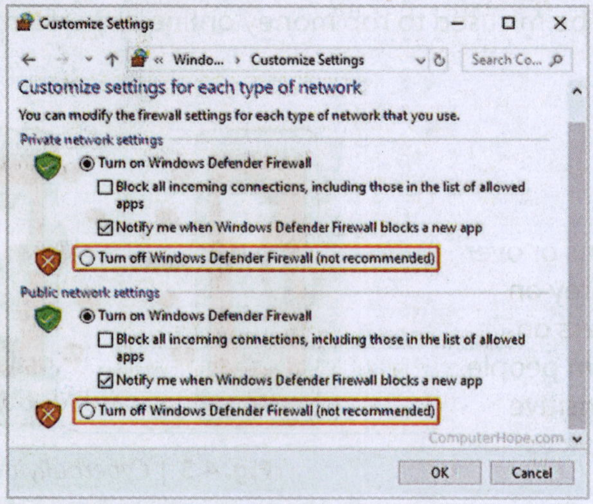

Fig. 4.6 | *Firewall settings on Windows 10*

Fig. 4.7 | *Antivirus*

2. **Check the URL**: A Uniform Resource Locator (URL) is required to open any website on the world wide web. A URL is like the address of the website. A secure website has a lock symbol before the URL and starts with HTTPS and not HTTP. HTTPS stands for HyperText Transfer Protocol Secure, and websites with HTTPS in their URL denote that they have additional security features as compared to the ones denoted by HTTP.

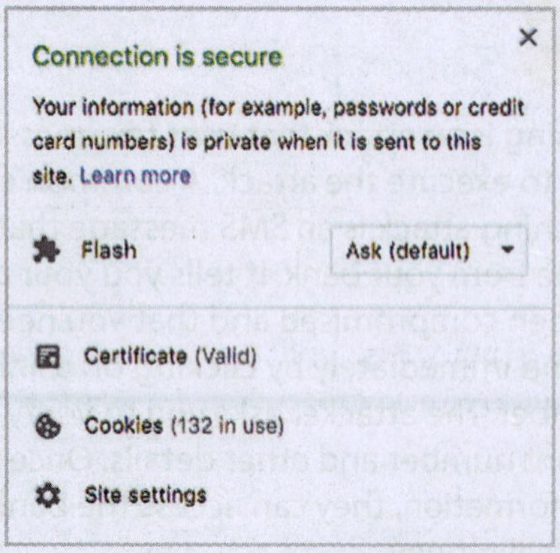

Fig. 4.8 | *A lock icon before the URL means secure connection*

Fig. 4.9 | *HTTP vs HTTPS*

3. **Be careful about clicking on links and downloading files**: Hackers often try to hack into the system by getting users to click on links or getting them to download files with malicious viruses. It could also be a prank link on an email. Before clicking on any link on any website, make sure it is trustworthy. Even if there is a slight doubt, refrain from clicking an unknown link or downloading a file.

Link up!

WhatsApp uses end-to-end encryption to secure its calls and messages.

4. **Beware of scams**: A scam is a method by which a cybercriminal lures people with free prizes in exchange for their financial details such as credit card numbers and bank account details. Misguided people, excited by the prospect, share their information, and money is stolen from their bank account. Always remember, nothing is sold on the internet for free, especially expensive things. Common scam themes are:
   - Fake shopping websites
   - Lottery
   - Work from home opportunities
   - Job offers
   - Free vacations

   Scam emails or posts are often worded incorrectly, show a sense of urgency or curiosity in clicking a link, and request personal information such as phone numbers or bank details.

Fig. 4.10 | *Scam website*

Brush up!

Which of the following URLs are secure? One has been done for you.

1. https://www.mindchamp.in Secure
2. http://umbrella.in ____________
3. https://www.nationalgeographic.com ____________
4. http://www.Mathsfun.io ____________
5. https://www.harpercollins.com ____________

5. **Be cautious while creating accounts on online platforms**: In today's world, it is inevitable that we create an email account or a social media account. Any type of account is our footprint on the web. Here's how we can be smart with them:
   - **Create strong passwords**: Have you seen this error message before? Why do websites encourage users to have strong passwords?

Passwords with only letters are simpler to decipher than passwords with numbers and symbols. This makes it more difficult for hackers to guess your passwords and break into your account. A strong password is at least 8-characters long and uses:

- Uppercase and lowercase letters, A–Z and a–z
- Numbers, 0–9
- Symbols, !@#$%^&*

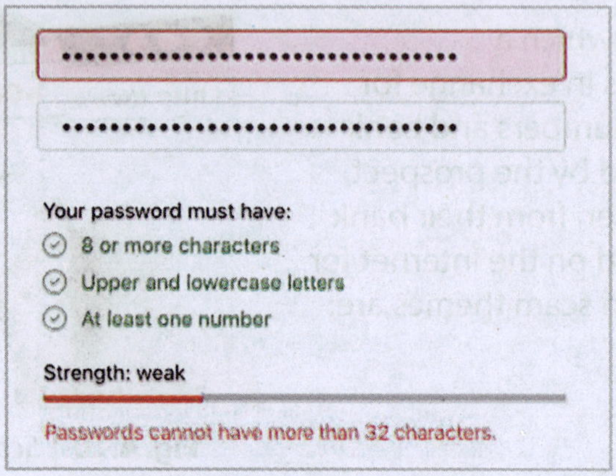

Fig. 4.11 | *Weak password*

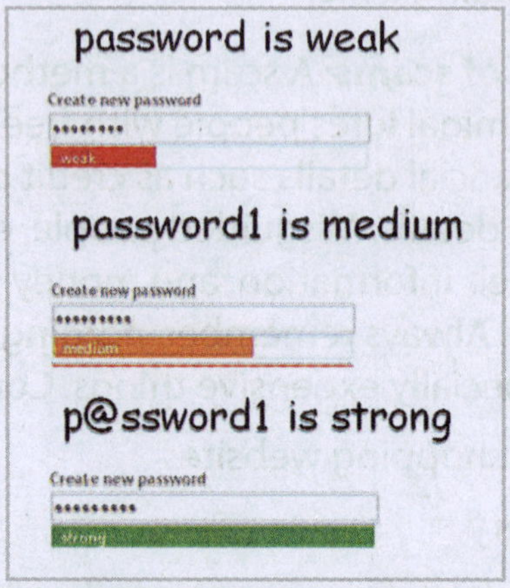

Fig. 4.12 | *Strong password*

Users often use simple passwords, such as names of family members so that they can remember it easily. However, it is not recommended. Thus, be it an email account, social media account, or even the Wi-Fi password, make sure it is protected with a strong password. Share your passwords only with your parents.

- **Manage Privacy Settings**: Usually, social media accounts allow users to post their personal information such as status, location, pictures, and so on. But, we have learned about impersonation and other threats that make a case for having strong privacy settings. Once an account is created, make sure only friends and family can access your information. Privacy settings are not only important for social media accounts but also for other sites where your personal information is stored. For example, in the phone settings, one can disallow Google to access their location.

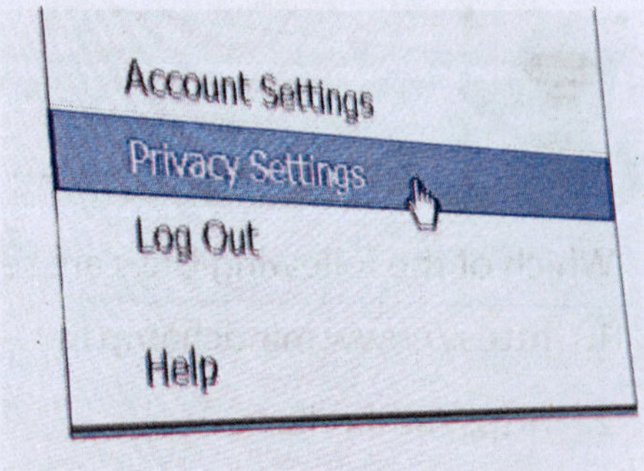

Fig. 4.13 | *Privacy Settings*

Fun with AI

AI-driven antivirus software can detect abnormalities in the system and help prevent attacks.

Another way of protecting data is to encrypt it. Encryption ensures that the data is not misused even if it falls into wrong hands. Recent experiments have demonstrated that AI-powered algorithms can be trained to encrypt data more effectively than traditional methods. Interestingly, these experiments also reveal that properly trained AI is better at encryption than decryption!

Clear up!

People post pictures of themselves, their family and friends on social media very often. Rajesh is no different. He posts pictures of food, meeting with friends on his social media account regularly. One of his friends has objected to Rajesh sharing her picture on the internet. What should Rajesh do? Is it incorrect to share the pictures or details about others on the internet without their permission? Why or why not?

Link up!

While setting up your Gmail account, did you notice that it asks you to enter an additional password or one-time pin (OTP) other than your username and password? Some applications require the user to provide two or more verification factors to gain access to a resource, such as an application, online account, or a VPN. This authentication method is called multi-factor authentication (MFA). This technique is used to decrease the risk of a successful cyberattack.

Communicating with Others Online

So far, we have learned about smart practices one should follow to have a safe online presence. The internet enables us to interact with many people, which is a reason for being responsible.

1. **Stick to limited and polite interactions**: Refrain from interacting with strangers on the web, unless from a reliable source. For example, someone unknown messaging on Facebook is not appropriate, but an Amazon delivery person might call you for delivery-related details. The delivery person's number is already provided by Amazon. Even while interacting with known people, make sure the language is polite and do not say anything inappropriate.

Fig. 4.14 | *Online interactions*

2. **Verify facts and give credit**: It is easy-to-share information at the click of a button; therefore, it is important to make sure it is not fake. Facts can be verified on official websites. Try to notice the difference between facts and opinions. For example, Rainfall levels higher than usual in Cherapunji" vs "Cherapunji facing extreme hardships due to heavy rainfall". The rainfall levels can be easily checked on the Meteorological Department's website. Cherapunji also gets rain throughout the year, so people have probably adapted to it.

Brush up!

Categorize the following passwords as strong, medium, or weak.

1. P+2001New
2. tommy
3. 20182019
4. Fb1234567
5. 123Cyber&girl
6. 1234456

Strong	Medium	Weak

Digital Footprints

We leave footprints from soiled shoes or wet feet. Footprints signify that a person walked that path. Every time, we connect to the internet to do anything, we leave a record of our activities. This record of activities is known as the digital footprint. Digital footprints signify the mark a person has left on various websites over the internet.

Digital footprints are the traceable trails of information left behind by a user on the internet. They are also known as digital shadows or electronic footprints.

Digital footprints are of two types:

- **Passive footprint**: Information left behind on the internet without the knowledge of users is known as passive footprints. Passive footprints do not contain the user's personal information. For example, many websites can know your approximate location. In this case, the website will know how many users visited their website from a particular city but not their names or contact details.

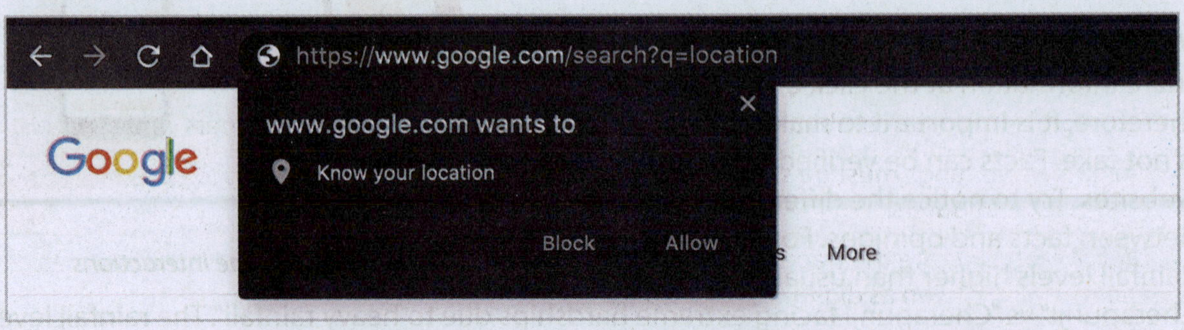

Fig. 4.15 | *Example of passive footprints*

- **Active footprints**: Active footprints refer to the information left on the internet with the awareness of the user. Emails and social media posts are examples of active footprints as others can see the identity of the person leaving the footprint. Therefore, it is better to be civil and courteous in all online interactions as information stays on the internet indefinitely.

A digital footprint is not a cause of concern till we practice ethical behaviour on the internet.

Link up!

A special division of the police called Cyber Security Police looks into solving and preventing cyber crimes, online frauds, etc. This division relies extensively on the digital footprint of suspects to track down criminals. Nowadays, police can track the location and movement of the suspects in the real time as well as see their past activities.

Brush up!

Social networking websites offer both risks and opportunities. List these here.

____

____

____

Today I learned!

- A person who uses the internet regularly is called a netizen or citizen of the internet.
- It is important to stay alert online because of threats such as hacking, fake news, fraud and impersonation.
- An antivirus is a software that protects computers from virus attacks.
- We should not click on suspicious links or download files from unknown sources to avoid scams.
- Always check for HTTPS that denots the URL of a secure website.
- Passwords must be a combination of uppercase and lowercase letters, numbers, and symbols.
- Our privacy settings must be strong enough to allow only family and friends to access information about us.
- Digital footprints are the traceable trails of information left behind by a user on the internet. They are also known as digital shadows or electronic footprints.
- Digital footprints are of two types: active and passive.

Revise and polish!

Learning Skills

1. Tick (✓) the correct answer.

a. Which of the following is the process of gaining unauthorized access to a computer system or an account?

(i) Scamming ☐ (ii) Bullying ☐ (iii) Hacking ☐ (iv) Phishing ☐

b. Which of the following refers to the information left on the internet with the awareness of the user?

(i) Active footprint ☐ (ii) Passive footprint ☐

(iii) Login ☐ (iv) Logout ☐

c. The 's' in https stands for:

(i) Safety ☐ (ii) Security ☐ (iii) Speed ☐ (iv) Secure ☐

d. A strong password contains:

(i) Numbers ☐ (ii) Letters ☐

(iii) Symbols ☐ (iv) All of the above ☐

e. In which form of cyberattack are users prompted into action via clickable links or phone numbers?

(i) Scamming ☐ (ii) Bullying ☐ (iii) Hacking ☐ (iv) Phishing ☐

f. Which of the following is a software (firmware) on the computer that prevents unauthorized access to a computer network or from it based on security settings?

(i) Firewall ☐ (ii) Fire safety ☐ (iii) Antiwall ☐ (iv) Antivirus ☐

g. Which of the following is a step towards ensuring safety while browsing the web?

(i) Checking the URL for HTTPS ☐

(ii) Installing an antivirus/firewall ☐

(iii) Being careful about clicking on links ad downloading files ☐

(iv) All of these ☐

h. The bombardment of unwanted information on the users is known as:

(i) Bullying ☐ (ii) Phishing ☐

(iii) Impersonation ☐ (iv) Spamming ☐

i. In which of the following attacks, the information seems to be from a trustworthy source?

(i) Bullying ☐ (ii) Phishing ☐

(iii) Impersonation ☐ (iv) Spamming ☐

j. Which of the following is a software that protects computers from virus attacks?

(i) Antivirus ☐ (ii) Malware ☐ (iii) Anti-theft ☐ (iv) Safety wall ☐

2. Fill in the blanks.

a. A citizen of the internet is called a ____________.

b. ____________ replicates itself in the computer and creates unwanted code.

c. A ____________ attack is where user data is stolen.

d. A URL with ____________ is more secure than a URL with HTTP.

e. A ____________ is a traceable trail of information left behind by the user.

3. Match the following.

a.	Weak password example	(i)	7+ninety1!
b.	Strong password example	(ii)	abc
c.	Scam	(iii)	"Click here to go to Hawaii for free!!"
d.	Firewall	(iv)	Location data
e.	Digital footprint	(v)	Prevents unauthorized access

4. Answer the following questions.

a. Explain Ethics in Computing in your own words.

b. Mention three reasons why being alert and smart while using the internet is important.

c. Is a strong password a necessity or a good-to-have? Give reasons.

d. Describe one illegal activity on the internet and a smart way to prevent it.

e. Explain Digital Footprints in your own words.

5. Solve the following puzzle.

Down:

1. Spreading false information on the web
2. Protects the computer network

Across:

3. Unauthorized access to a computer
4. Laws on safety over the internet
5. Set photos privacy settings for only friends and family

Think and Answer

What should be the ideal response in the following situations?

1. Nisha gets the following email. Should she claim her lottery winnings?

   Hello! You have been selected for a ₹1 crore lottery!!! Hurry up and send your contact details on this link to claim the money. Hurry up before it expires!!

   ____

   ____

2. Your father receives the following SMS from an unknown number. What would you advise him to do?

   Hi…. I am your childhood friend… I am in urgent need of funds: (Please send me money urgently I am waiting…..)

   ____

   ____

3. On social media, you come across the following link: http://spaceastronomy12345.com. Would you visit the website?

   ____

   ____

4. A cousin or sibling of yours is creating their first social media account. What are two things you would advise them to be cautious about?

   ____

   ____

Chapter

5

Spreadsheets—An Introduction

After reading this chapter, I will be able to:

- ✔ Define a spreadsheet.
- ✔ List the features of a spreadsheet.
- ✔ Create a worksheet.
- ✔ Identify the components of the spreadsheet window.
- ✔ Differentiate between a workbook and a worksheet.

Brainstorm and explore!

Information Literacy

Ganesh started a new restaurant and stored all the customer details and purchases in his book. Within a year, the place started getting more than 100 customers per day, and the numbers kept increasing on a daily basis. Seeing the increase, Ganesh started storing all the information on a computer, instead of the books. Why do you think he stopped using the books?

____

____

____

Ganesh now stores all those records in a spreadsheet application on his computer. Just like books, a spreadsheet can store lots of data that can be updated regularly, is easy to store, does not occupy a lot of space, and will not get lost. Examples of a spreadsheet application include MS Excel, OpenOffice Calc and Google Spreadsheets.

In this chapter, we will be learning about MS Excel 2016 in detail.

spreadsheet application: a computer program with inbuilt features and tools designed to store and analyse large amounts of data

Starting MS Excel 2016

Just like MS Word and MS PowerPoint, MS Excel is part of the Microsoft Office suite. It can be used to store, edit and analyse large amounts of data with ease.

The two ways to start MS Excel are given below:

1. Click the **Start** button on your desktop.
2. In the Start menu, look for and click on the **Excel** option (Fig. 5.1).

OR

Press the Windows key (⊞)+R to start the Run program, then type 'excel' and click the **OK** button (Fig. 5.2).

The MS Excel 2016 application window will open.

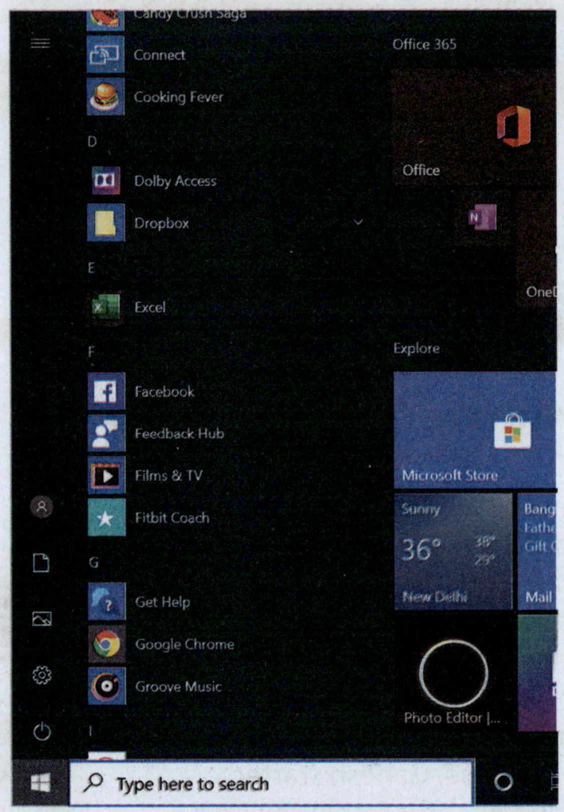

Fig. 5.1 | *Starting MS Excel 2016 using the Start menu*

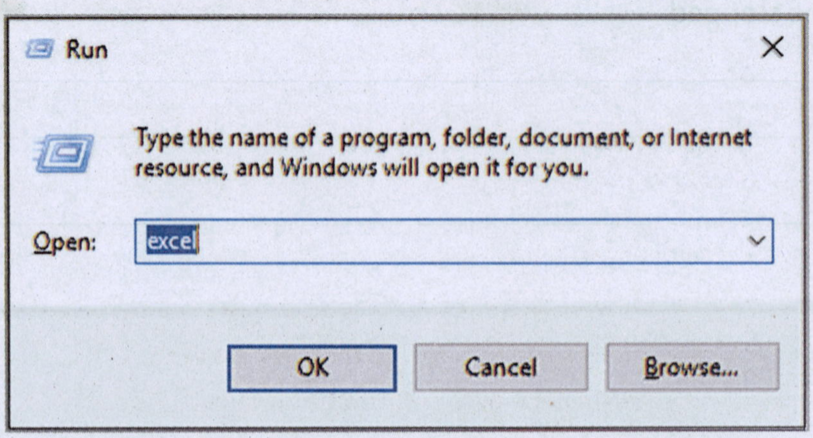

Fig. 5.2 | *Starting MS Excel 2016 using the Run program*

Components of the Spreadsheet Window

The MS Excel window opens with a new workbook which has one worksheet (Sheet 1) by default. The various components of the MS Excel 2016 window are shown in Fig. 5.3 and discussed here.

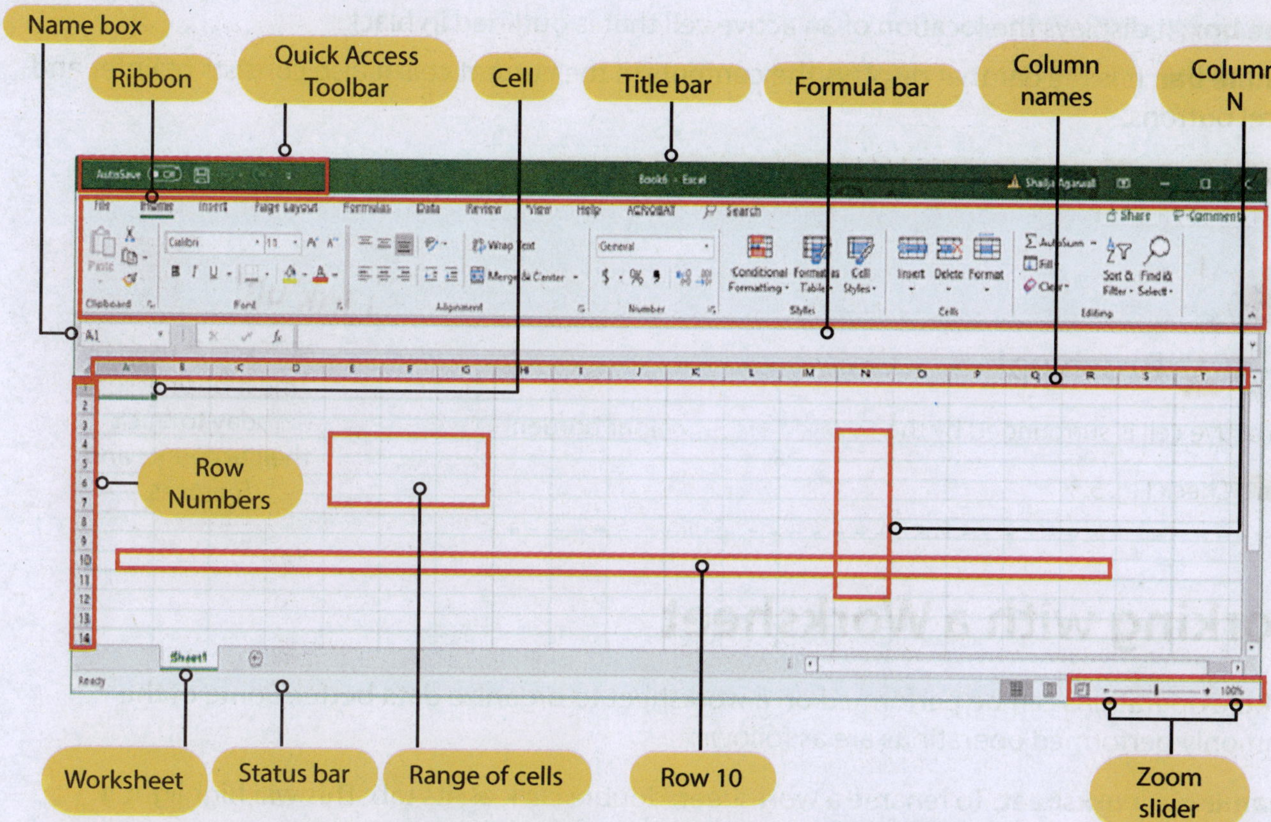

Fig. 5.3 | *Components of MS Excel 2016 window*

Quick Access toolbar, Ribbon, Title Bar, Status Bar and Zoom Slider perform the same functions as discussed while learning about other Microsoft applications.

The components specific to Microsoft Excel 2016 are discussed below:

Worksheet: It is the work area arranged in horizontal rows and vertical columns. It is like a page of your Math notebook. You may add or delete worksheets. You may change the name of the worksheet. Each worksheet consists of 10,48,576 rows and 16,384 columns.

A collection of one or more worksheets stored under a single file name is called a **workbook**. We should store related worksheets in the same workbook to keep them together. The first file opened by default is a **blank workbook**.

Columns: It is an arrangement of cells in the vertical direction. Microsoft Excel uses letters to label columns. The columns are labelled from left to right starting with A, B, C … Z for the first 26 columns and AA to AZ …. XFD for the remaining columns.

Rows: It is the arrangement of cells in the horizontal direction. Microsoft Excel uses numbers to label rows. The rows are numbered from top to bottom starting from 1, 2, 3, …., 576.

Cell: It is the intersection of a column and a row. It is the basic unit of a worksheet.

An **active cell** is the selected cell in which data is entered when you begin typing. Only one cell is active at a time. The active cell is the highlighted cell surrounded by a border. Data can only be entered into an active cell. As per Fig. 5.3, A1 is the active cell.

Cell address: It is the address used to identify a cell. The very first cell, where column A and row 1 intersect, is referred to as A1. This is the cell address. The column label always comes first and then the row number.

Range of cells: It is the group of cells adjacent to each other, forming a rectangular shape.

Name box: It displays the location of an active cell that is outlined in black.

Formula bar: It is the bar that displays the contents in the current cell. It also consists of Enter and Cancel buttons.

adjacent: next to something else, sharing a common border

Brush up!

An active cell is surrounded by the ____________ colour border.

Hint: Check Fig. 5.3

Link up!

MS Excel is used by most businesses today to track their accounts and finances.

Working with a Worksheet

Multiple operations can be performed on a worksheet to organize data better. Some of the commonly performed operations are as follows:

Renaming a worksheet: To rename a worksheet, double click on its tab. This will highlight it. Type the new name and the **Enter** key.

Adding a new worksheet: To add a new worksheet in addition to the default worksheet, click on ⊕ button near the worksheet tab.

Deleting a Worksheet: To delete a worksheet, right-click on it and click on **Delete** in the menu that appears.

To move between various worksheets, click on the respective worksheet tabs.

Saving a Workbook

After creating a workbook in MS Excel, the steps to save it are:

1. Click on the **File** tab and select the **Save As** option.
2. Select the location where you wish to save the file in the **Save As** dialog box.
3. Type the name of the file in the **File name**: text box, and click on the **Save** button (Fig. 5.4). A new file named Book1.xlsx will be created in the selected folder.

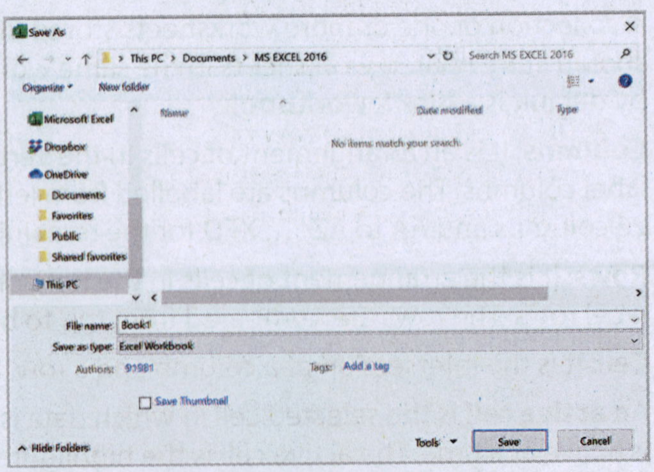

Fig. 5.4 | *Save As dialog box*

Soak up!

Prior to Excel 2007, the default file extension was .xls. These files can still be used in Excel 2016.

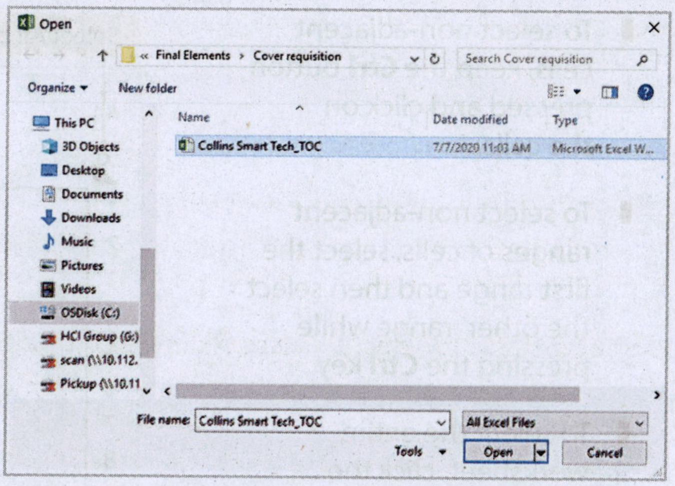

Fig. 5.5 | *Open dialog box*

Opening an Existing Workbook

If the MS Excel application window is already open, we can open an existing file by following the steps given below:

1. Click on the **File** tab and select the **Open** option.
2. In the Open dialog box (Fig. 5.5), locate the file you want to open, then click on it. Once the file is selected, the name of the file will be displayed in the **File name**: text box.
3. Click on the **Open** button and the workbook will be displayed in the application window.

Soak up!

A workbook is the name given to an Excel file and contains one or more worksheets or sheets.

To open a workbook when the MS Excel window is not open, double-click on the file in the folder that contains it.

Selecting Cells and Modifying Cell Contents

The method of selection of data in MS Excel depends on the range of cells to be selected.

The selected portion is enclosed within a thick black border. The cell selected in Fig. 5.6. is A1.

- To select a single cell, click on it.
- To select an entire row or column, click on the corresponding row heading (1) or column heading (A), as shown in Fig. 5.7.

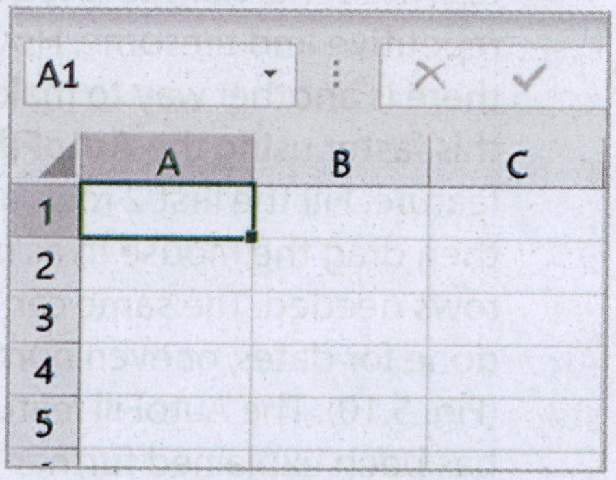

Fig. 5.6 | *Selecting a single cell*

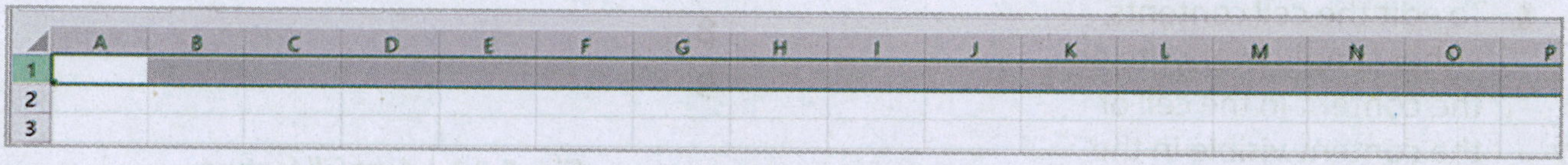

Fig. 5.7 | *Selecting an entire row*

- To select non-adjacent cells, keep the **Ctrl** button pressed and click on the cells.
- To select non-adjacent ranges of cells, select the first range and then select the other range while pressing the **Ctrl** key.
- To select the entire worksheet, click the **Select All** button at the intersection of the row and column headers or press **Ctrl+A** (Fig. 5.8).

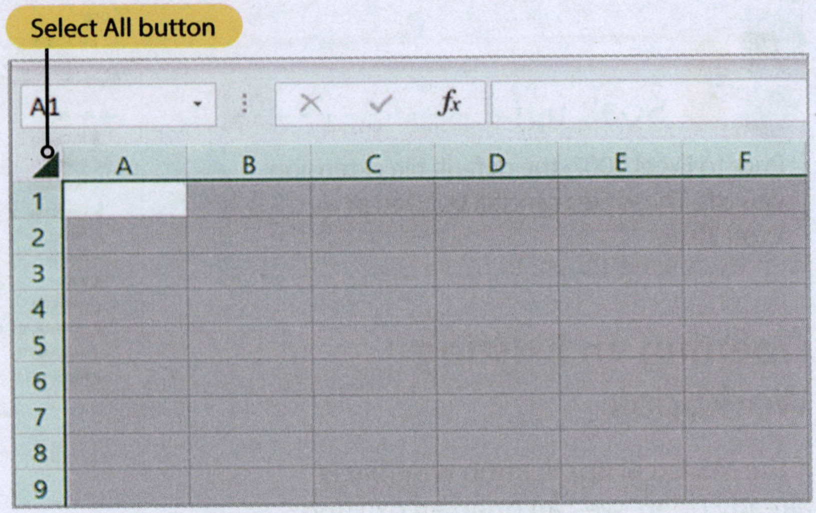

Fig. 5.8 | *Selecting the entire worksheet*

- To autoFill the same content in the adjacent cells, click on the first cell (a bold plus symbol will appear), and then, click and drag the mouse pointer up to the last cell you want to have the content. Release the button to complete the selection (Fig. 5.9).

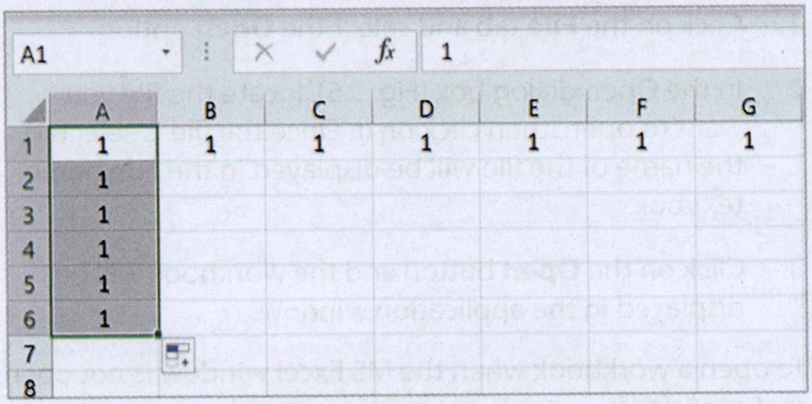

Fig. 5.9 | *Using AutoFill Feature for filing similar content*

- Sometimes, when you want to write serial numbers, it gets repetitive and tiresome. However, there is another way to make this faster using the **AutoFill** feature. Fill the first 2 rows and then drag the mouse to as many rows needed. The same can be done for dates, or even numbers (Fig. 5.10). The AutoFill feature has been explained further in the next chapter.

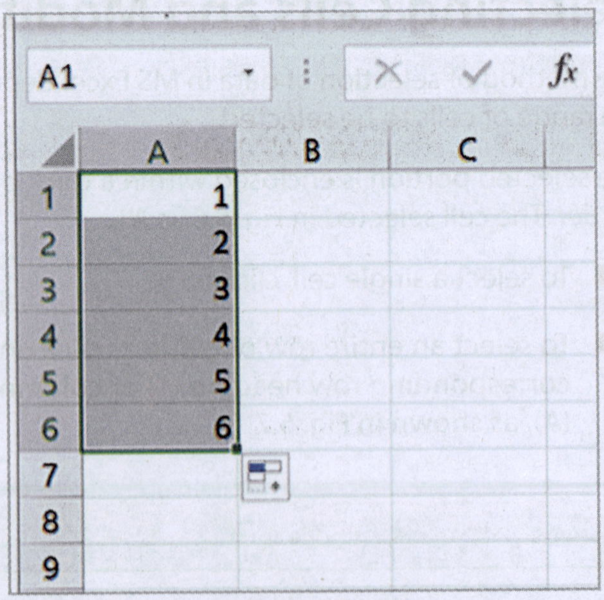

Fig. 5.10 | *AutoFill feature*

- To edit the cell contents, either simply overwrite on the content in the cell or the content visible in the **Formula bar**.

Deleting Cell Contents

To delete cell contents, either use the **Delete** key on the keyboard or follow the steps given below:

1. Select the cell or the range of cells to be deleted.
2. Right-click and select **Clear Contents** from the menu that appears (Fig. 5.11).

Once the content is deleted, we can start writing new content in the cells.

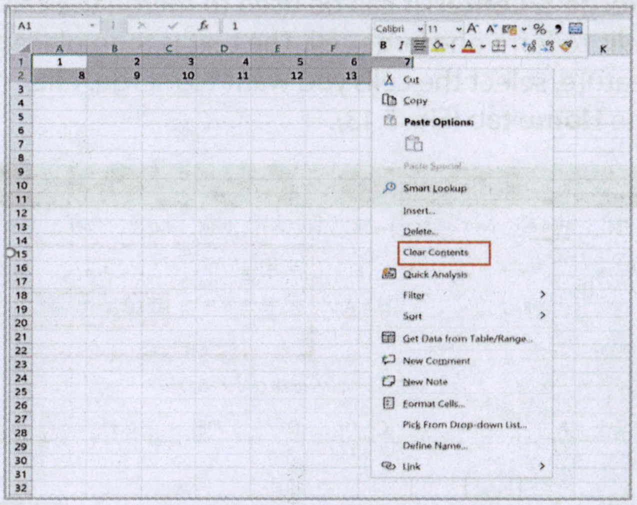

Fig. 5.11 | *Deleting cell contents*

Soak up!

We can align the text in the cells as well as increase or decrease the indent in the alignment group.

Containing Text in a Single Cell

When the text is too long to fit in a single cell, it extends to adjacent cells. This extended portion is not visible if the adjacent cell contains data. To solve this problem, MS Excel provides the following two features.

Wrap Text: It allows us to fit the content within the same cell by displaying it in multiple lines. To use this feature, select the cell and click on **Wrap text** in the **Alignment** group under the **Home** tab (Fig. 5.12).

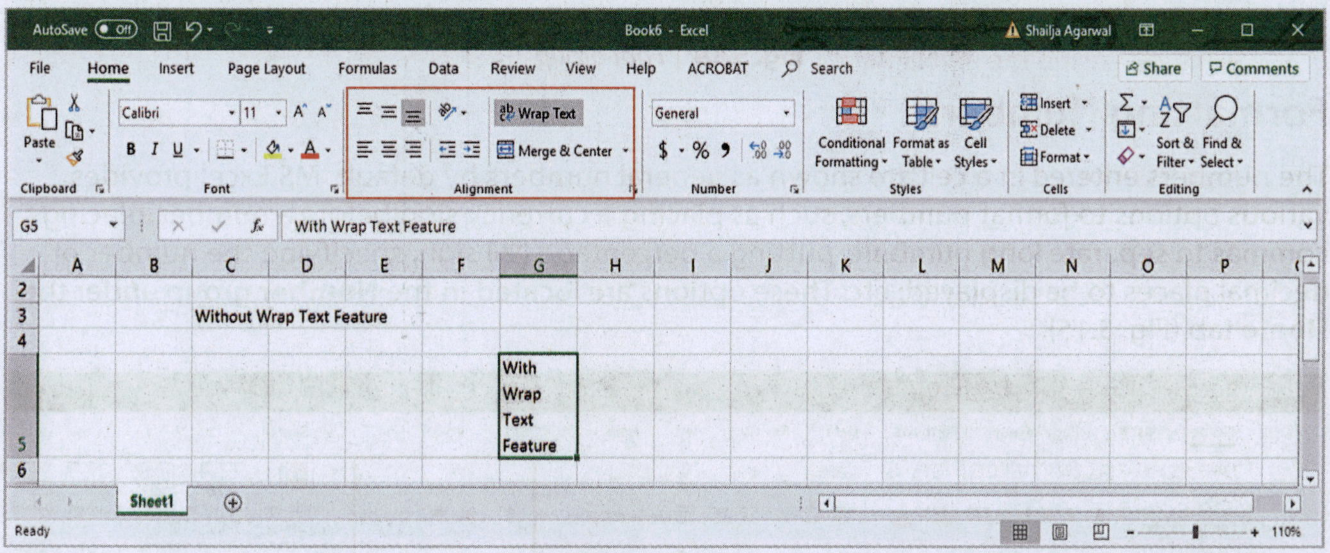

Fig. 5.12 | *Wrap Text*

Merge & Center: It can be used to merge the cell containing long text with one or more adjacent cells to form one large cell. The text is then placed at the center of the merged cells. To use this feature, select the cells you want to merge. Click on **Merge & Center** in the **Alignment** group under the **Home** tab (Fig. 5.13).

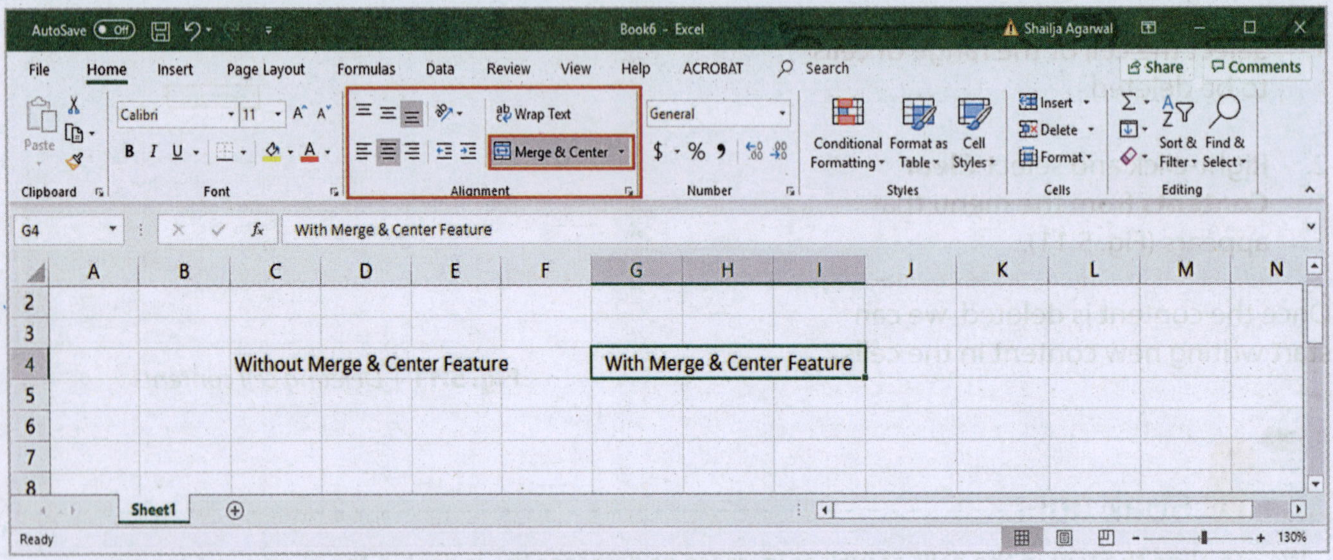

Fig. 5.13 | *Merge & Center*

Formatting Text and Numbers in Excel

The **Font** group under the **Home** tab contains the options for formatting text (Fig. 5.14). From here, we can change the font style, size, colour, background colour, border style, etc.

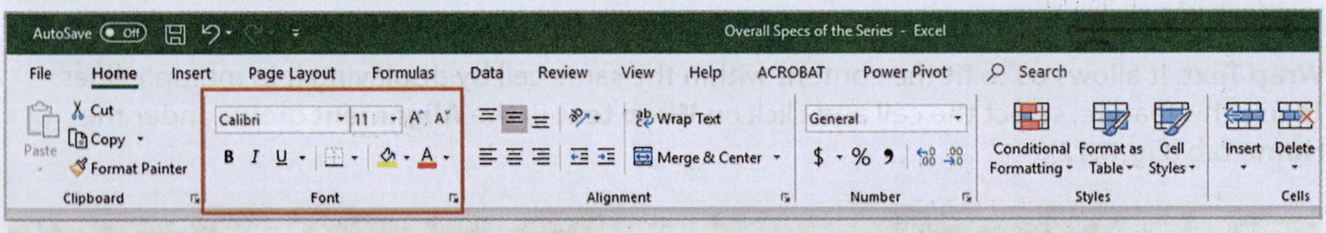

Fig. 5.14 | *Font group*

Formatting Numbers

The numbers entered in a cell are shown as general numbers by default. MS Excel provides various options to format numbers, such as placing a currency sign before a number, placing commas to separate long numbers, putting a percentage (%) sign, specifying the number of decimal places to be displayed, etc. These options are located in the **Number** group under the **Home** tab (Fig. 5.15).

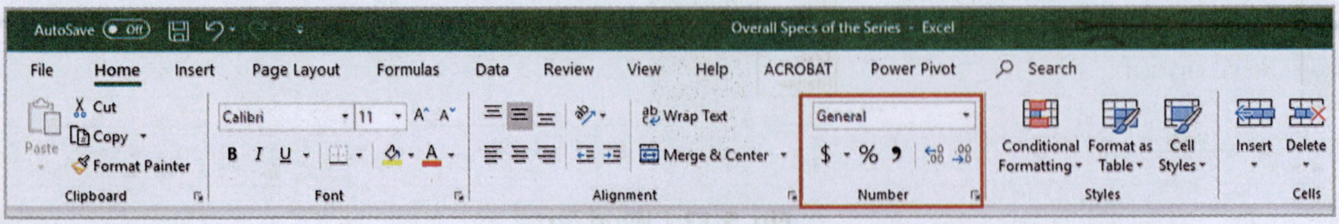

Fig. 5.15 | *Number group*

The **Number** group gives a drop-down list with various options in which the values in the cells can be displayed as percentage, fraction, date/time, etc.

- The **Percentage Style (%)** button changes the number to its percentage form.
- The **Comma (,)** button adds commas separating the thousands in the number.

For example, we can change the number format to add two decimal numbers by following the steps given below:

1. Select the cell for which you want to change the format.
2. Click on the drop-down arrow in the **Number** group under the **Home** tab (Fig. 5.16).
3. Click on the **Number** option from the drop-down list. You will notice that the number is changed to a decimal number.

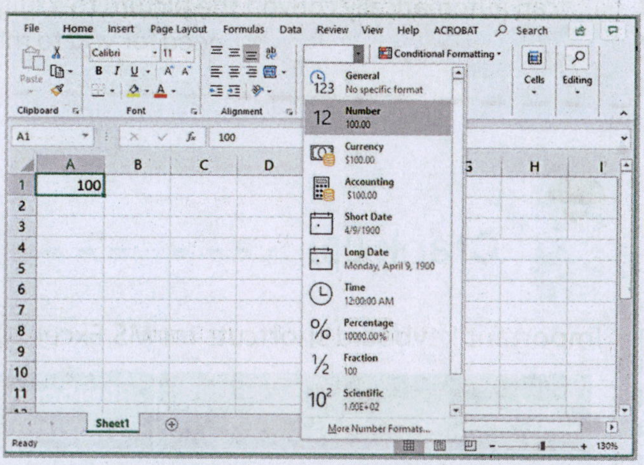

Fig. 5.16 | *Number group of buttons*

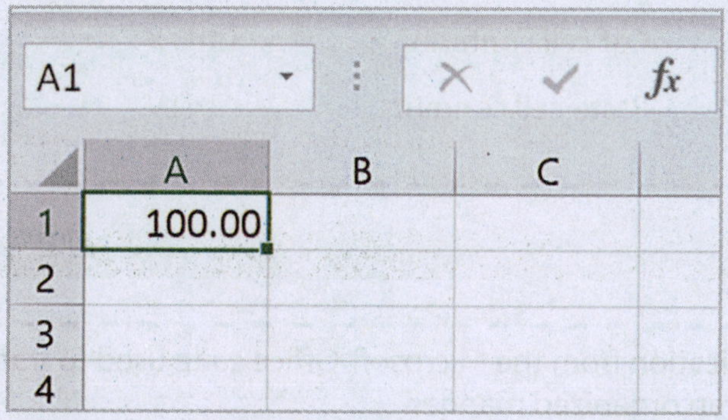

Fig. 5.17 | *Number with two decimal places*

Clear up!

How can you add ₹ in front of a number as shown alongside?

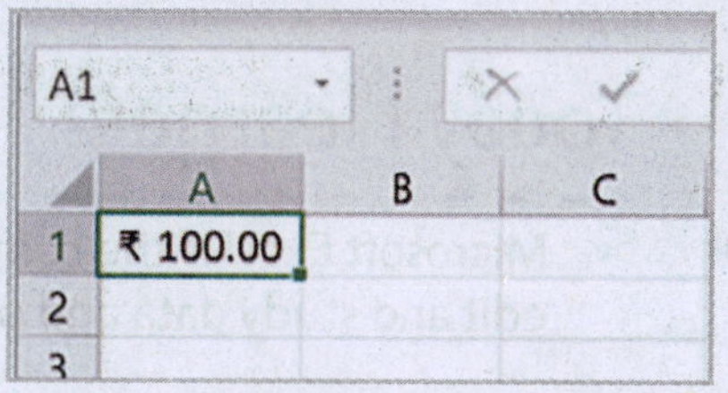

Exiting MS Excel 2016

To exit the MS Excel application, click on the Cross (X) button located at the top right corner of the application window. Or, click on the **File** tab and then select the **Close** option.

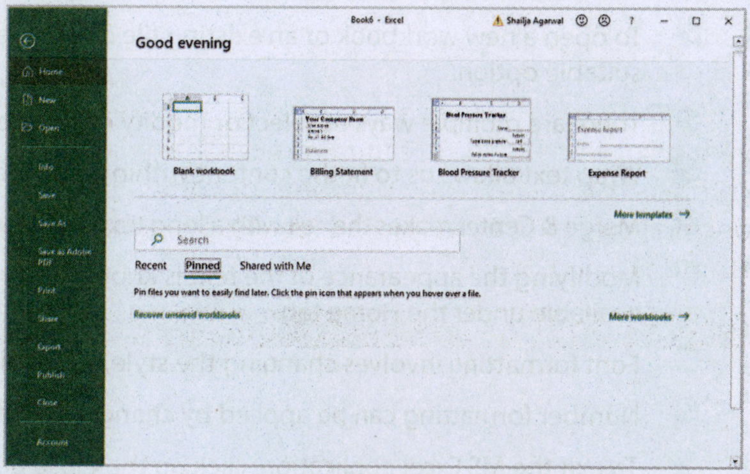

Fig. 5.18 | *Exiting MS Excel*

Fun with AI

Inserting data with pictures is a new image recognition functionality introduced in MS Excel, which can automatically convert the picture to a fully editable table in a an worksheet, eliminating the need for you to manually enter the data.

Crank up!

Technology Literacy

Important keyboard shortcuts for MS Excel 2016 are given below:

Action	Keyboard Shortcut	Action	Keyboard Shortcut
Open a new workbook	Ctrl+N	Select an entire column	Ctrl+Spacebar
Save a workbook	Ctrl+S	Select an active row	Shift+Spacebar
Select the entire workbook	Ctrl+A	Copy cell contents	Ctrl+C
Open an existing workbook	Ctrl+O	Cut cell contents	Ctrl+X
Close the MS Excel application	Alt+F4	Paste cell contents	Ctrl+V

Today I learned!

- Microsoft Excel is the computer application from the Microsoft Office suite used to track, edit and study data and present it in an organized manner.
- Some of the important components of MS Excel 2016 application window are the Title bar, Formula bar, Rows and Columns, Name box, Ribbon and Status bar.
- To open a new workbook or an existing file or to save a file, click on the File tab and select the suitable option.
- There are multiple ways to select or modify cell content.
- Wrap text allows us to fit the content within the same cell by displaying it in multiple lines.
- Merge & Center makes the cell with a long text merge with the adjacent cells and form one large cell.
- Modifying the appearance of the text is known as formatting. All the formatting options are available under the Home tab.
- Font formatting involves changing the style, size and colour of the font.
- Number formatting can be applied by changing the format in which numbers are displayed.
- To exit the MS Excel application, click on the Close button.

Revise and polish!

Learning Skills

1. Tick (✓) the correct answer.

a. What is a workbook?

(i) A group of cells ☐ (ii) A group of rows ☐

(iii) A group of worksheets ☐ (iv) A group of columns ☐

b. Which of the following steps should be followed to make a big cell by combining two or three cells?

(i) Home → Merge & center ☐ (ii) Insert → Wrap text → Merge ☐

(iii) Page layout → Merge ☐ (iv) All of these ☐

c. Akash wants to create a table for the scores achieved by students. While typing "Name of the Students", he noticed that the text could not be accommodated within a cell. In this case, for creating a proper table what should he do?

(i) Wrap the text ☐ (ii) Merge all the surrounding cells ☐

(iii) Change the font type ☐ (iv) Change the font type ☐

d. How the width of a cell can be increased?

(i) By dragging the rows of the cell ☐ (ii) By dragging the column of the cell ☐

(iii) By wrapping ☐ (iv) All of these ☐

e. How to add a new worksheet in an existing spreadsheet?

(i) Go to Insert tab and then click on the table. ☐

(ii) Click on the Review tab. ☐

(iii) Click on the Insert Worksheet option. ☐

(iv) Click on the Insert tab ☐

f. The symbol for "Insert Worksheet" is located at ____________ of Excel window.

(i) Top right ☐ (ii) Bottom left ☐

(iii) Bottom right ☐ (iv) Centre ☐

g. In a new spreadsheet, how many worksheets are visible by default?

(i) 3 ☐ (ii) 2 ☐

(iii) 1 ☐ (iv) 4 ☐

h. In a spreadsheet, letters are used to represent ____________.

(i) Columns ☐ (ii) Rows ☐

(iii) Cells ☐ (iv) Worksheets ☐

i. The cell that is being use is called the ______.

(i) highlighted cell ☐ (ii) main cell ☐

(iii) active cell ☐ (iv) Any cell ☐

j. Which of the following statements is true, if the current or active cell is B4 and you have pressed the Enter key?

(i) You will be in the cell A1 ☐ (ii) You will be in the cell B5 ☐

(iii) You will be in the cell B3 ☐ (iv) You will be in the cell B6 ☐

2. Fill in the blanks.

a. To select non-adjacent ranges of cells, select the first range and then select the other range while pressing the ______________ key.

b. Spreadsheet is a grid of ______________ and columns.

c. 21-03-2022 date format can be added by selecting ______________ from the Number group.

d. To select an entire row, click on the selected ______________ heading.

e. To close a workbook in MS Excel, click on the ______________ tab and then click on Close.

f. The ______________ of a workbook in MS Excel is .xlsx by default.

3. Match the following.

a.	MS Excel 2016	(i)	Spreadsheet application
b.	Google spreadsheets	(ii)	Blank worksheet
c.	Title bar	(iii)	MS Office suite
d.	Clear contents	(iv)	Displays name of a worksheet
e.	Ctrl+N	(v)	Deletes cell content

4. State whether the following statements are true (T) or false (F).

a. Merge text allows us to fit the content within the same cell by displaying it in multiple lines. ☐

b. Shortcut to close an application is Alt+F1. ☐

c. Formatting options are available in the Home tab. ☐

d. Background colour of one cell can be changed. ☐

e. AutoFill feature automatically fills the adjacent cells. ☐

5. What does each of the keyboard shortcuts do?

a. Ctrl+A ______________ b. Ctrl+V ______________

c. Shift+Spacebar ______________ d. Shift+Tab ______________

e. Ctrl+Z ______________ f. Ctrl+S ______________

6. **Give the steps for the following activities in MS Excel.**
   a. Opening and closing an existing worksheet
   b. Fill a row with dates of next month using AutoFill
   c. Deleting a cell content

7. **Answer the following questions.**
   a. What is the difference between a workbook and a worksheet?
   b. What is Formula bar?
   c. What do you mean by a 'range of cells'?
   d. Define the following terms.
      (i) Navigating worksheet
      (ii) Insert cells and rows
      (iii) Drag and drop
      (iv) Workbook protection

Lab Activities

1. Create a worksheet, type the name of your favourite cartoon/game character in the cell A1 and format text according to the instructions given below:
   a. Change the font style to Times New Roman
   b. Change the font size to 14
   c. Make the text bold
   d. Add a border on all four sides
   e. Save the document

   What is the extension it gets saved as? ___________

2. Create a worksheet to store records of all students in your class. Insert minimum three columns of your own choice (For example, Serial Number/Hobby/Age/Address/DOB, etc.).

   Make sure the cell contents are formatted correctly.

3. Create a worksheet to store records of all the subject marks you obtained in your class. Choose a minimum 3 columns of your own choice. For example, Serial Number, Subjects, Marks, Total Percentage/CGPA.

   Make sure the cell contents are formatted correctly.

4. Create a spreadsheet template for calculating the total price of all ice cream flavours (chocolate, strawberry, vanilla, etc.) for all the students. You need to add the price for all the flavours and calculate the total amount.

Hint: You can refer to the following sheet or create your own spreadsheet.

A	B	C	D	E	F
Name:					
	Favorite Ice Cream Flavour				
	Chocolat	Vanilla	Strawber	Other	Total
Students					

Chapter

6

More About Spreadsheets

After reading this chapter, I will be able to:

- ✔ Define the features of a spreadsheet.
- ✔ Discuss the different types of data (number, string and formula).
- ✔ Explain how to enter and edit data in a spreadsheet.
- ✔ Tell the use of the Autofill feature.
- ✔ Explain how to move data in a spreadsheet.
- ✔ Differentiate between the different ways to perform calculations.
- ✔ Understand creating and editing a formula and performing calculations with formula.
- ✔ Modify a worksheet and insert and delete columns and rows in a worksheet.

Brainstorm and explore!

Mrs. Janhavi is a teacher who has to create a report card for 45 students of her class. She has to insert the name of each student and marks obtained by them in 5 different subjects. Mrs. Janhavi also has to find total marks for each student and then rank them accordingly.

Which software application do you think she should use to fill in all the details?

____

What are the different fields that she should add in the report card?

____

Do you think the total should be done separately for every student using a calculator?

____

We have learned in the last chapter that spreadsheets in MS Excel are useful in entering, editing, analyzing and storing data. This data can be preset in the form of text, numbers or a combination of both. Arithmetic operations with numerical data such as addition, subtraction, multiplication and division can be done using MS Excel for numbers only.

Features of MS Excel

Some important features of MS Excel are discussed below:

1. **Formatting**: The cells which one selects can be formatted to represent different numeric values in a spreadsheet. This is beneficial for different data sets, such as finance and accounts. For such data sets, formatting the spreadsheet will place decimals and commas to show dollar and cent symbols. Thus, the inserted data looks uniform and the operations, such as merging, inserting or deleting data become quicker.
2. **Rows and columns**: The spreadsheet in MS Excel is arranged in a grid of rows and columns. This makes all the information appear neatly organized in one easy-to-read space.
3. **Formulas and functions**: MS Excel allows us to use a lot of in-built functions and formulas. It also allows us to write and use our own formulas. This feature helps us perform calculations on our data.
4. **Pivot tables**: These tables help us analyze complex data relationships graphically. Pivot tables can flip and/or put together large data in seconds. They help us in data analysis and generate reports with the help of the analysed data. Pivot tables are used to create periodic financial statements, statistical reports, etc.
5. **Data filtering and visualizations**: MS Excel offers some enhanced filtering and sorting techniques to arrange data and/or to find the desired answers in a worksheet quickly. Some examples of filters are sort by color, sort by date, display more than 1000 items in the AutoFilter drop-down list, select multiple items to filter, filter data using Pivot tables, etc.

Types of Data

We can use different types of data in an MS Excel spreadsheet. Some of these are discussed here:

1. **Numbers**: Numbers can be from the entire range of numeric values: whole numbers (example, 25), decimals (example, 25.67) and scientific notation (example, 0.2567E+2). Excel displays scientific notation automatically to enter a number that is too long to be viewed in its entirety in a cell. We may also see number signs (# # # # # #) when a cell entry is too long. Widening the column that contains the cell with the above signs will allow reading the number.
2. **Text**: First, select the cell in which data has to be entered and type the text. Press the **Enter** key to finish the text entry. The text will be displayed in the active cell as well as in the **Formula bar**. If the numbers to be treated as text, use an apostrophe (') as the first character. The calculations cannot be done with this kind of data entry.
3. **Formula**: A formula is an equation that performs a calculation. Formulas help perform mathematical calculations in the worksheet. They always begin with equal to (=) sign followed by cell addresses, operators and numbers. We will learn about this in detail further in the chapter.

Entering Data in a Spreadsheet

Let us begin building the workbook by manually entering data into a worksheet.

Consider the example of Mrs. Janhavi's class discussed earlier. The following steps explain how the column headings in Row 1 are typed into the worksheet:

1. Click on the cell location A1 in the worksheet.
2. Type "SUBJECT" in A1.
3. While typing, the data appears both in the worksheet and in the Formula bar, as shown in Fig. 6.1.

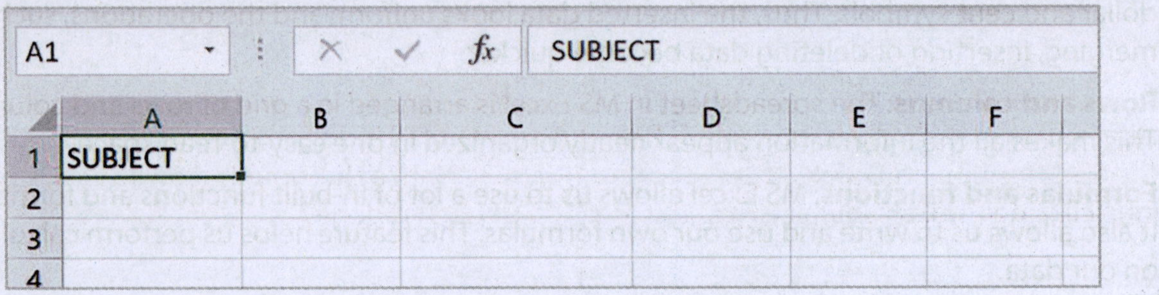

Fig. 6.1 | *Typing data in the cell A1*

4. Press the right arrow key (→). This will activate the next cell A2.
5. Type "MARKS" in A2 and press the right arrow key (→) again.
6. Repeat step 5 for the word PERCENTAGE and then again for CGPA.

Figure 6.2 shows how the worksheet should appear after entering the column headings in Row 1.

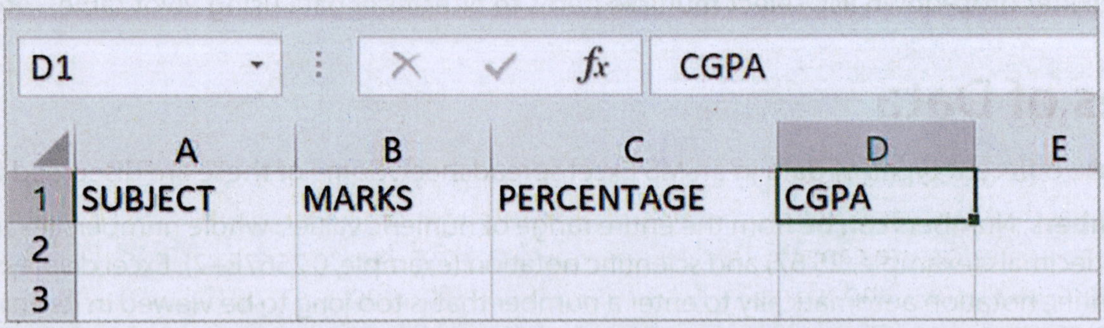

Fig. 6.2 | *Entering column headings into a worksheet*

Editing Data

Data entered in a cell can be changed by double-clicking the cell location or using the Formula bar. The Formula bar can be used for entering data into cells, as well as for editing data that already exists in a cell.

The steps to edit data are as follows:

1. To delete particular data, select the cell containing the data and then press the **Delete** key.

2. To replace data, just select the cell and retype the correct data. The newly entered data will replace the old data in the cell.

3. To bring back the previous entry, either click on the **Undo** option on the **Standard Toolbar**, as shown in Fig. 6.3, or go to **Edit** → **Undo**.

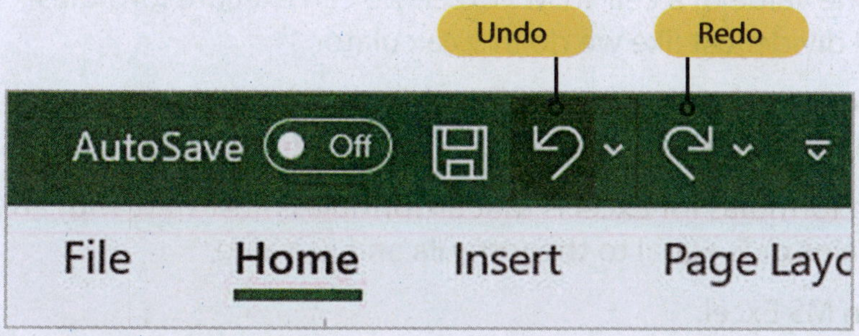

Fig. 6.3 | *Undo and redo options in the Standard toolbar*

Crank up! Technology Literacy

The keyboard shortcut to undo content in a cell is Ctrl+Z.
The keyboard shortcut to redo content in a cell is Ctrl+Y.

Sometimes, we accidentally undo our last action. To undo the **Undo** command, select the text and click the **Redo** option on **Quick Access Toolbar** (Fig. 6.3). Notice that your last undo was reverted. Continue clicking until all your accidental undo(s) have been redone.

Clear up!

Radhika is a student of Mrs. Janhavi's class. Radhika noticed that her score of English was not entered correctly in her marksheet. So, she requested the teacher to change her marks.

Which feature should Mrs. Janhavi use to make that change in the spreadsheet she has created?

____

AutoFill

The **AutoFill** feature allows us to quickly fill cells with repetitive or sequential data such as chronological dates or numbers and repeated text. This feature can also be used to copy functions. It can be used to alter text and numbers with this feature. Following are the steps to use the AutoFill feature to enter the days of the week in Column A of a worksheet.

1. Select cell A2 in the Sheet1 worksheet.
2. Type the word "Monday" and press the Enter key.
3. Activate cell A2 again.
4. Move the mouse pointer to the lower right corner of cell A3. Notice a small square in the corner of the cell; this is called the **Fill Handle** (Fig. 6.4). When the mouse pointer gets close to the Fill Handle, the white block plus sign will turn into a black plus sign.

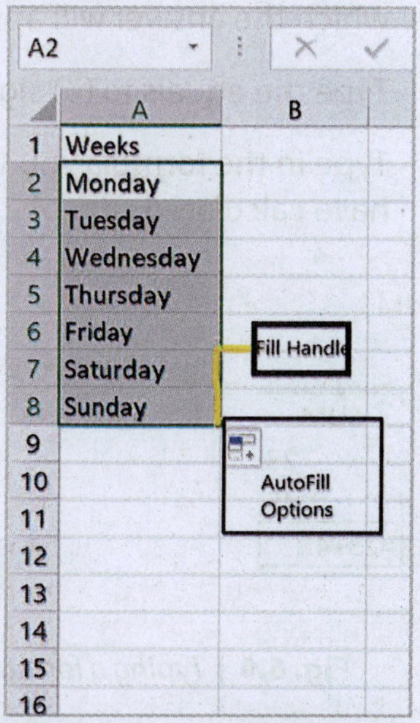

Fig. 6.4 | *Using Autofill to enter the days of the week*

Left-click and drag the Fill Handle to cell A8. Notice that the AutoFill tip box indicates what day will be placed into each cell (Fig. 6.4). Release the left mouse button when the tip box reads "Sunday."

Simple Formulas

A **formula** is an expression that calculates the value of a cell. In MS Excel, we can execute formulas that can help us add, subtract, multiply and divide just like we do in a calculator.

MS Excel uses standard operators for equations, such as a plus sign for addition (+), minus sign for subtraction (–), asterisk for multiplication (*), forward slash for division (/) and caret (^) for exponents.

The key thing to keep in mind when writing formulas for Excel is that all formulas must start with an **equal sign** (=). This is because the cell contains or is equal to the formula and its value.

Table 6.1 shows the arithmetic operations in MS Excel.

Table 6.1 | *Arithmetic operations in MS Excel*

Kind of operation	Operator	Operation	Example
Arithmetic	+	Addition	=A2+B3
	–	Subtraction	=A3–A2 or –C4
	*	Multiplication	=A2*B3
	/	Division	=B3/A2
	^	Exponentiation	=A2^3

Creating a Simple Formula

1. To calculate the sum of 23 and 45, select the cell in which the answer will appear (let us say A4).
2. Type the equals to (=) sign.
3. Type in the formula you want MS Excel to calculate. We have calculated sum of 23 + 45, as shown in Fig. 6.5.

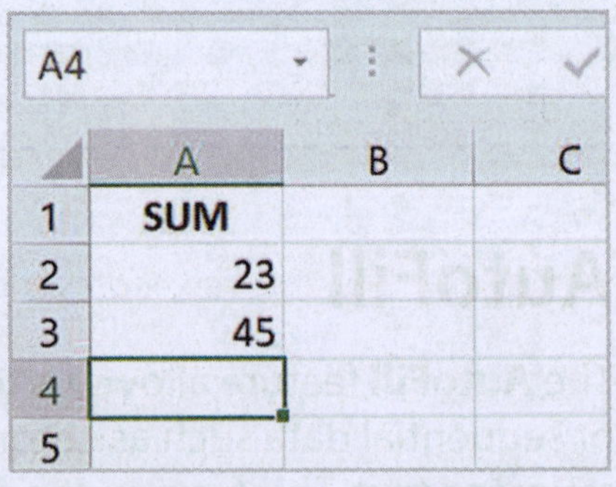

Fig. 6.5 | *Selecting a cell*

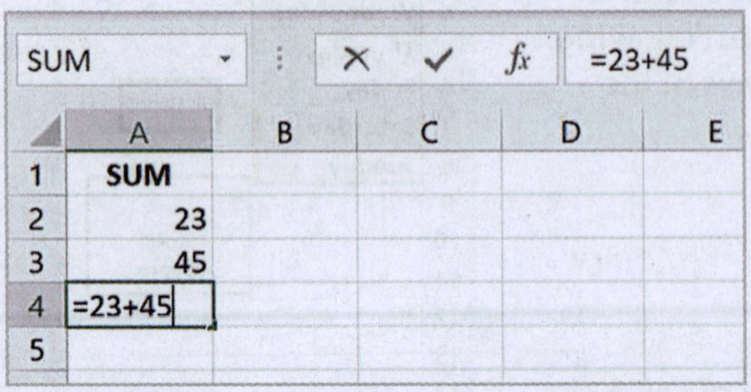

Fig. 6.6 | *Typing a formula in the cell*

4. Press the Enter key. The formula will be calculated, and the value will be displayed in the cell (Figs. 6.6 and 6.7).

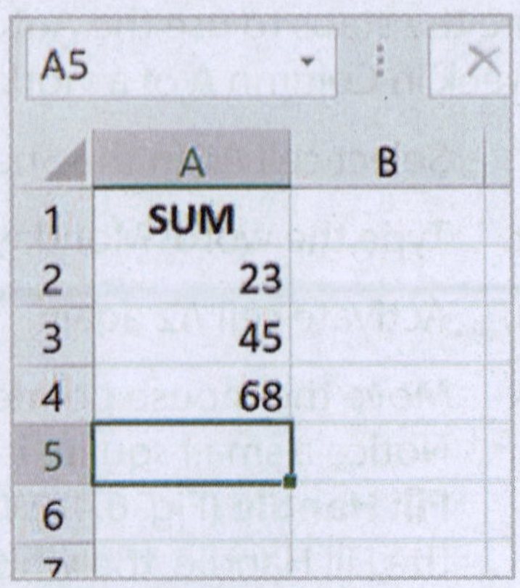

Fig. 6.7 | *Calculated value*

Creating Formulas with Cell References

When a formula contains a cell address, it is called a **cell reference**. Creating a formula with cell references helps update data in the worksheet without having to rewrite the values in the formula.

The steps for creating a formula using cell references are given below:

1. To multiply 23 from 45, select the cell where the answer will appear (Let us say A4).
2. Type the **equals sign (=)**.
3. Type the cell address that contains the first number in the equation (A2, as shown in Fig. 6.8).

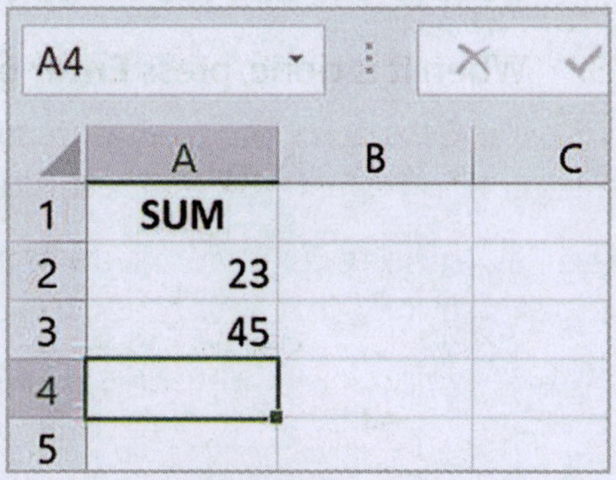

Fig. 6.8 | *Selecting a cell*

4. Type the operator for the formula. For example, type the multiplication sign (*).
5. Type the cell address that contains the second number in the equation (Let us say A3) (Fig. 6.9).

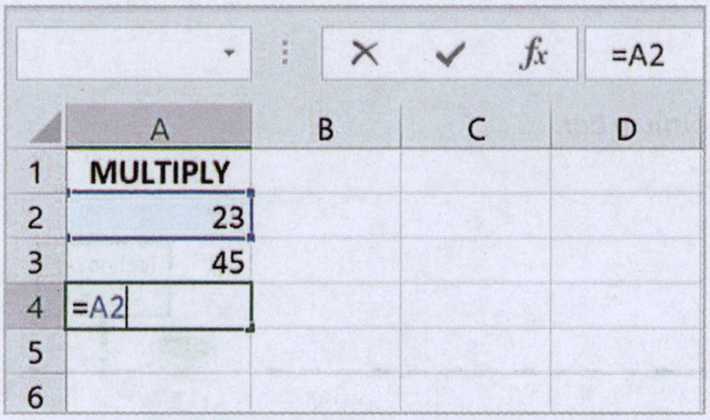

Fig. 6.9 | *Typing Cell Address of First Number*

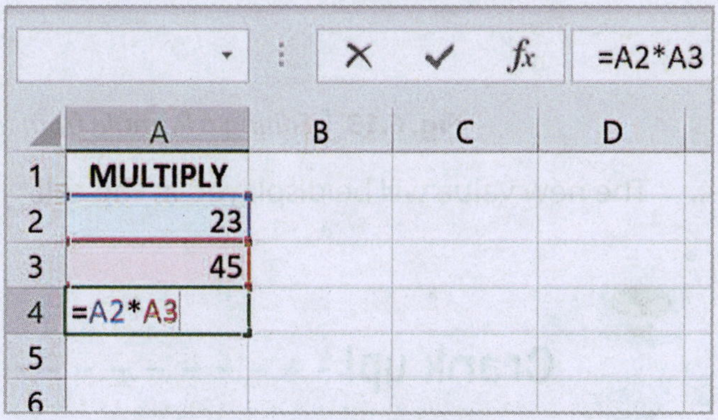

Fig. 6.10 | *Operator for the Formula*

6. Press the **Enter** key. The formula will be calculated, and the value will be displayed in the cell (Figs. 6.10 and 6.11).

If there is a change in value of either A2 or A3, the total will automatically be recalculated (Fig. 6.12).

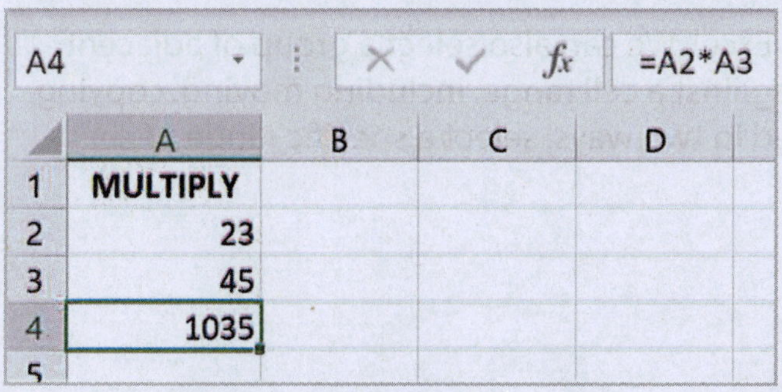

Fig. 6.11 | *The calculated value*

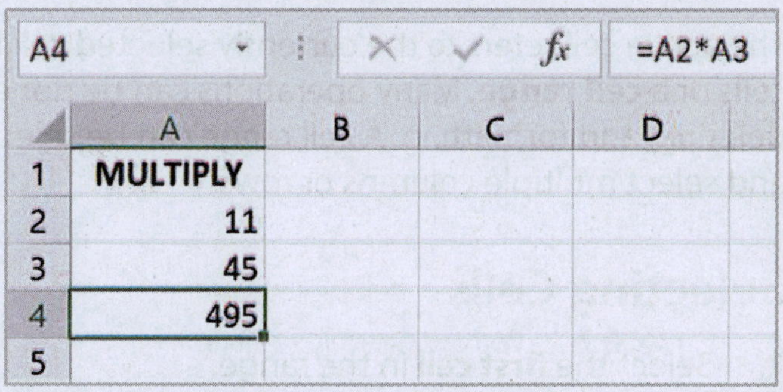

Fig. 6.12 | *Automatic recalculation*

Editing a Formula

1. Select the cell that needs to be edited.
2. Insert the cursor in the **Formula bar**, and edit the formula as required. Another way is by **double-clicking the cell to view and edit the formula directly** from the cell (Fig. 6.13).
3. When it is done, press **Enter** or select the **Enter** command.

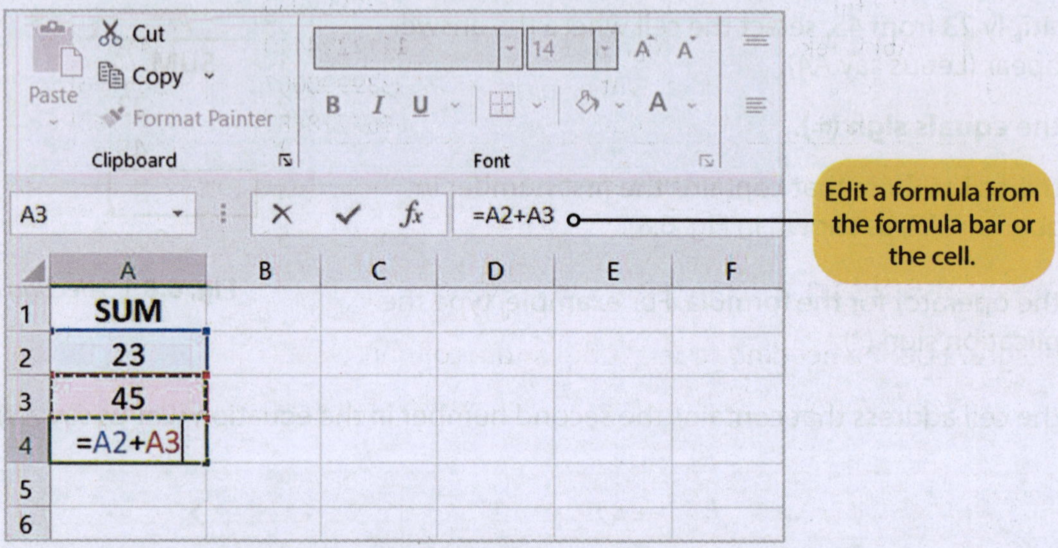

Fig. 6.13 | *Editing a formula from the Formula bar*

4. The new value will be displayed in the cell.

Crank up!

To change the previous edit, use the **Cancel** command ☒ in the formula bar to avoid accidentally making changes to the formula.

Selecting Multiple Cells

The active cell refers to the currently selected cell in Excel. We can also select a group of adjacent cells or a **cell range**. Many operations can be done against a cell range, including moving, copying, deleting, and formatting. A cell range can be selected in two ways: select a specific range of cells and select multiple columns or rows.

Selecting Cells

1. Select the **first cell** in the range.
2. The mouse pointer becomes a **large cross**.

3. Click and hold the left mouse button and **drag** left or right, up or down to the last cell to select.
4. Now, release the mouse button. The selected cells will appear shaded (Fig. 6.14).

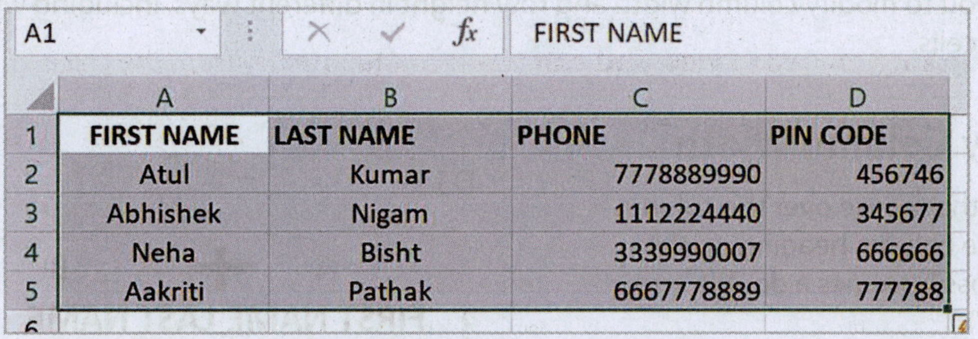

A1 | FIRST NAME

	A	B	C	D
1	FIRST NAME	LAST NAME	PHONE	PIN CODE
2	Atul	Kumar	7778889990	456746
3	Abhishek	Nigam	1112224440	345677
4	Neha	Bisht	3339990007	666666
5	Aakriti	Pathak	6667778889	777788

Fig. 6.14 | *Selecting multiple cells*

Selecting All Cells in a Column or a Row

1. Click the grey column heading to select the entire column.
2. Select the grey **column** heading to select the entire column. Click and drag the cursor across other column headings to select those columns (Fig. 6.15).

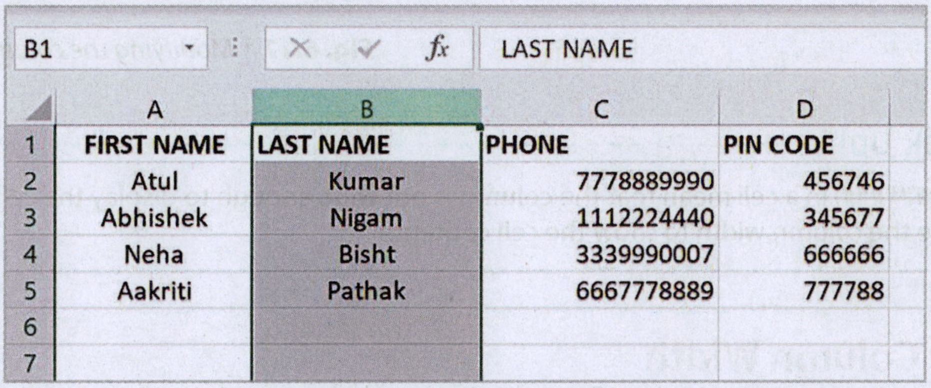

B1 | LAST NAME

	A	B	C	D
1	FIRST NAME	LAST NAME	PHONE	PIN CODE
2	Atul	Kumar	7778889990	456746
3	Abhishek	Nigam	1112224440	345677
4	Neha	Bisht	3339990007	666666
5	Aakriti	Pathak	6667778889	777788
6				
7				

Fig. 6.15 | *Selecting all cells in a column*

3. Select the grey **row** heading to select the entire row (Fig. 6.16). Click and drag the cursor down through the row headings to select those rows.

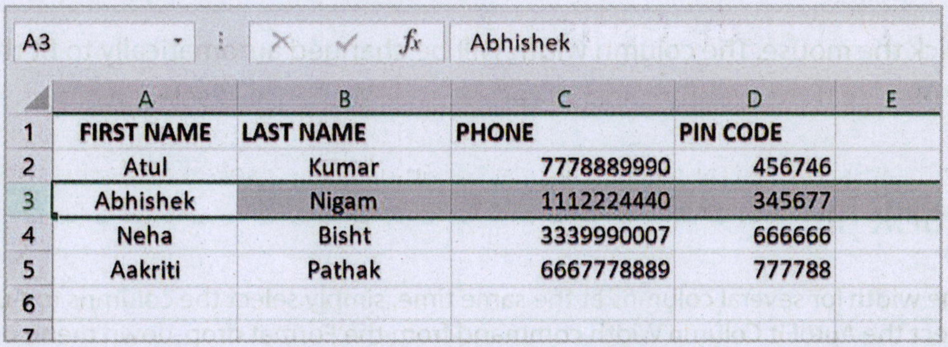

A3 | Abhishek

	A	B	C	D	E
1	FIRST NAME	LAST NAME	PHONE	PIN CODE	
2	Atul	Kumar	7778889990	456746	
3	Abhishek	Nigam	1112224440	345677	
4	Neha	Bisht	3339990007	666666	
5	Aakriti	Pathak	6667778889	777788	
6					

Fig. 6.16 | *Selecting all cells in a row*

Modifying a Worksheet

By default, every row or column of a new workbook is always set to the same height and width. Excel allows you to modify column width and row height in different ways, including wrapping text and merging cells.

To Modify Column Width

1. Position the mouse over the column line in the column heading, so the white cross becomes a double arrow (Fig. 6.17).
2. Click, hold and drag the mouse to increase or decrease the column width.
3. Release the mouse button. The column width will be resized.

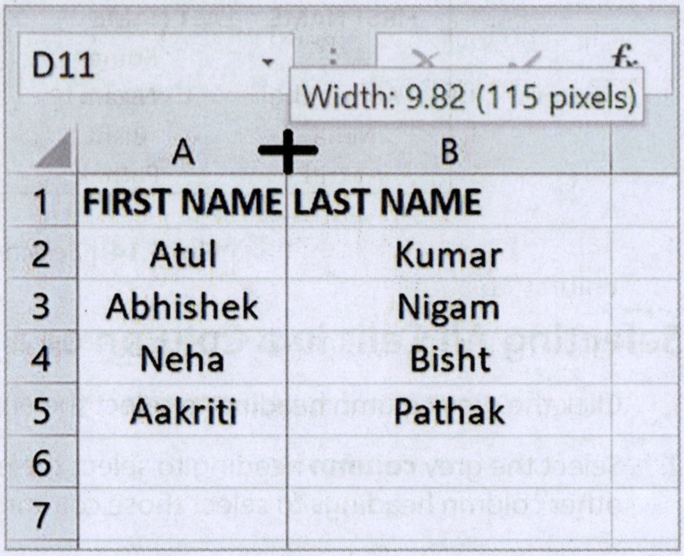

Fig. 6.17 | *Modifying the column width*

Soak up!

Pound signs (#######) in a cell mean that the column is not wide enough to display the cell content. Simply increase the column width to show the cell content.

To AutoFit Column Width

The AutoFit feature will allow setting a column's width to fit its content automatically.

1. Position the mouse over the column line in the column heading so the white cross becomes a double arrow.
2. Double-click the mouse. The column width will be changed automatically to fit the content.

Technology Literacy

Crank up!

To AutoFit the width for several columns at the same time, simply select the columns to AutoFit and then select the AutoFit Column Width command from the Format drop-down menu on the Home tab. This method can also be used for Row height.

Inserting, Deleting and Moving Rows and Columns

Inserting Rows

1. Select the row heading below where you want the new row to appear.
2. Click the **Insert** command on the **Home** tab (Fig. 6.18).
3. The new row will appear above the selected row.

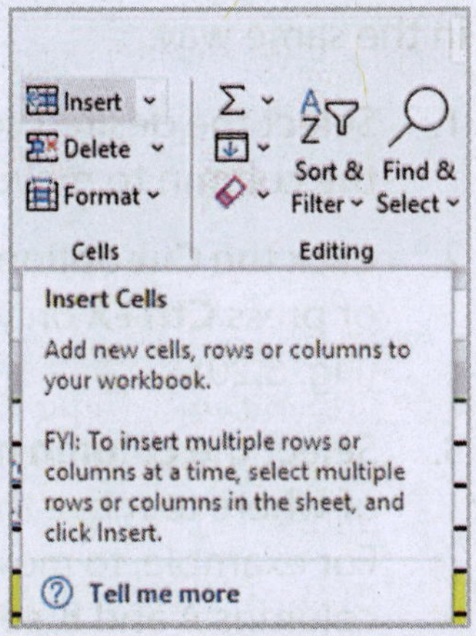

Fig. 6.18 | *Inserting rows and columns*

Inserting Columns

1. Select the column heading to the right of where you want the new column to appear.
2. Click the **Insert** command on the **Home** tab.
3. The new column will appear to the left of the selected column.

When inserting rows and columns, make sure to select the entire row or column by clicking the heading. If you have selected only a cell in the row or column, the Insert command will only insert a new cell.

Deleting Rows

It is easy-to-delete any row that you no longer need in your workbook.

1. Select the row(s) you want to delete.
2. Click the **Delete** command on the **Home** tab (Fig. 6.19).
3. The selected row(s) will be deleted, and the rows below will shift up.

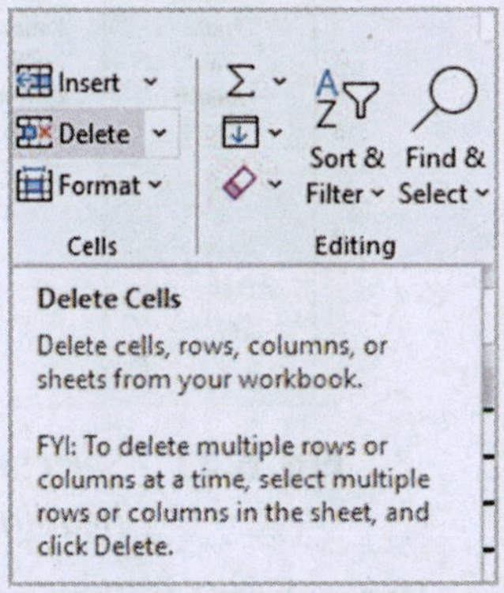

Fig. 6.19 | *Deleting rows and columns*

Deleting Columns

1. Select the column(s) you want to delete.
2. Click on the **Delete** command on the **Home** tab.
3. The selected column(s) will be deleted, and the columns to the right will shift left.

Soak up!

It is important to understand the difference between deleting a row or column and simply clearing its contents. To remove the content of a row or column without causing others to shift, right-click a heading, and then select Clear Contents from the drop-down menu.

Moving a Row or Column

To move a row or column refer to below steps. Here, we will move a column, but we can move a row in the same way.

1. Select the desired **column heading** for the column to move.
2. Click the **Cut** option on the **Home** tab or press **Ctrl+X** on your keyboard (Fig. 6.20).
3. Select the **column heading** to the left of where to move the column (Fig. 6.21). For example, to move a column between columns A and B, select **column A**.

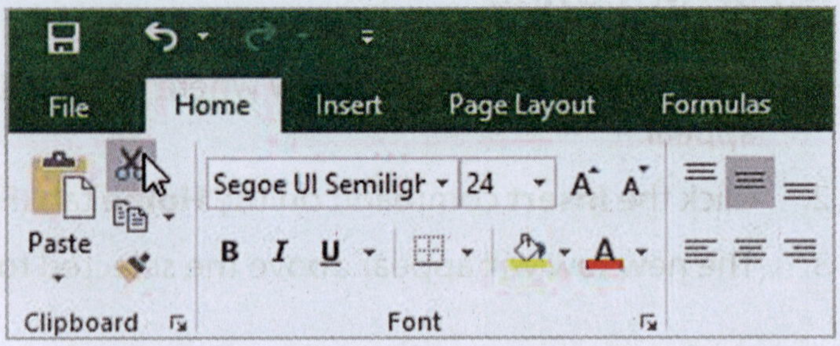

Fig. 6.20 | *Selecting the option from the Home tab*

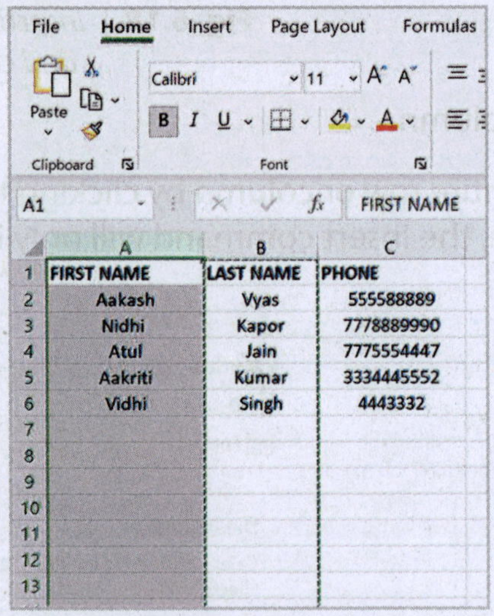

Fig. 6.21 | *Selecting column heading B to move*

4. Click the **Insert** command on the **Home** tab and then select **Insert Cut Cells** from the drop-down menu (Fig. 6.22).

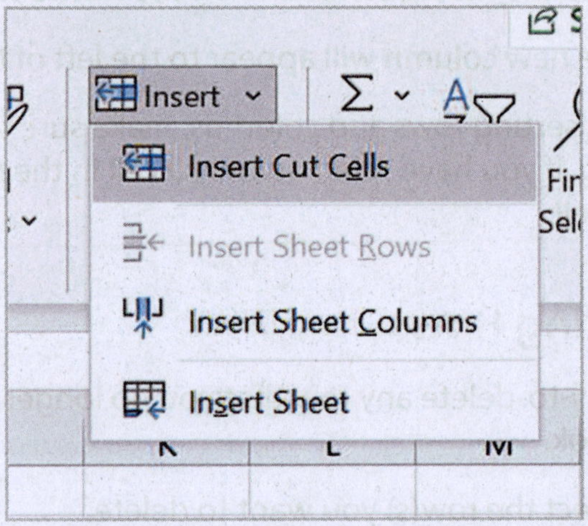

Fig. 6.22 | *Inserting cut cells*

5. The column will be moved to the selected location (Fig. 6.23).

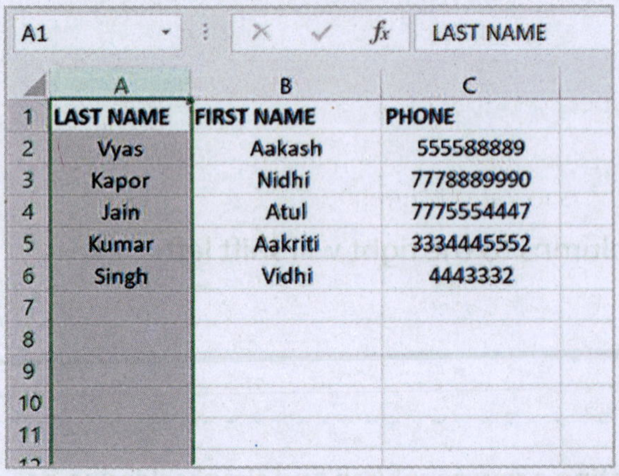

Fig. 6.23 | *Column moves to the desired location*

Crank up!

One more way to access the **Cut** and **Insert** commands by right-clicking the mouse and selecting the **desired commands** from the drop-down menu.

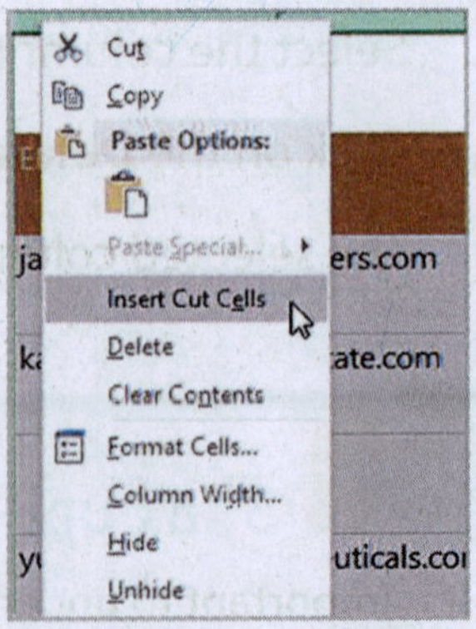

To copy a column, follow the same steps and click on the **Copy** option on the **Home** tab. After selecting the column, you can also press the shortcut key Ctrl+C to copy the column.

Brush up!

Give the steps for moving and copying a column in Excel. Also explain the difference between the two.

____

____

____

____

____

____

Today I learned!

- Some important features of spreadsheets in MS Excel are formatting, rows and columns, formulas and functions, pivot tables, data filtering and visualization.
- We can use different types of data such as numbers, text and formula in a spreadsheet.
- The AutoFill feature allows us to quickly fill cells with repetitive or sequential data such as chronological dates or numbers and repeated text.
- Formulas are the user-defined instructions to perform calculations such as addition, subtraction, multiplication, division, etc.
- A formula sets a relationship between two or more cells. It can include cell addresses, arithmetic operators, numbers and parentheses.
- A formula must begin with an equal to (=) symbol, followed by cell reference and operator.
- Operators are symbols like +, -, ^, %, *, #, etc.
- A cell range can be selected in two ways: select a specific range of cells or select multiple columns or rows.
- We can insert, delete, copy or move rows and columns in a worksheet.

Revise and polish!

1. Tick (✓) the correct answer.

a. Which one of the following is not a function of MS Excel?

(i) AVERAGE ☐ (ii) ADD ☐ (iii) MAX ☐ (iv) MIN ☐

b. Look at the following sheet with the cost of different instruments.

How is the total cost per year for all the instruments calculated?

(i) By adding cells C7 through E7 ☐

(ii) By adding cells C2 through C6 ☐

(iii) By adding cells E2 through E6 ☐

(iv) By adding cells D2 through D6 ☐

	A	B	C	D	E
1	Name	Instrument	Fee per Month	Number of Months	Total Cost
2	Dhanush	Sexophone	₹45.00	10	₹450.00
3	Kiran	Guitar	₹35.00	10	₹350.00
4	Samrat	Trumpet	₹60.00	5	₹300.00
5	Rohan	Drums	₹55.00	0	₹00.00
6	Bharat	Flute	₹42.00	0	₹00.00
7			Total Rental Fee		₹1100.00
8					

c. What are predefined formulas in MS Excel called?

(i) Parentheses ☐ (ii) Operators ☐ (iii) Function ☐ (iv) Range ☐

d. Which command allows the user to reverse the last action?

(i) Redo ☐ (ii) Undo ☐ (iii) Repeat ☐ (iv) Copy ☐

e. Which error is obtained when a formatted number does not fit within a cell?

(i) ##### ☐ (ii) #DIV@ ☐ (iii) #VALUE! ☐ (iv) #DIV/0 ☐

f. What is the function of MAX( )?

(i) It finds the average value of the given cell range. ☐

(ii) It finds the minimum value of the given cell range. ☐

(iii) It finds the maximum value of the given cell range. ☐

(iv) It finds the sum value of the given cell range. ☐

g. What is the shortcut key combination of redo function?

(i) Ctrl+Z ☐ (ii) Ctrl+Y ☐ (iii) Ctrl+X ☐ (iv) Ctrl+P ☐

h. Which feature of MS Excel helps you enter a series of data automatically?

(i) AutoFill ☐ (ii) Auto sum ☐ (iii) Function ☐ (iv) AutoAdd ☐

i. Which of the following statements is false?

(i) You cannot format a number to currency in MS Excel. ☐

(ii) Steps to align contents of the cell are: Format → Cells → Alignment tab ☐

(iii) Font style can be changed by using buttons of the standard toolbar. ☐

(iv) All of these ☐

j. What is the use of the AutoComplete feature of Excel?

(i) It automatically completes abbreviated words. ☐

(ii) It completes text and numeric entries that match an existing entry in the same column. ☐

(iii) It completes text entries that match an existing entry in the same column. ☐

(iv) All of these ☐

2. Fill in the blanks.

a. A formula starts with an ____________ sign.

b. By default, a workbook contains ____________ worksheets.

c. A spreadsheet cell that is highlighted with a heavy border is called an ____________.

d. What will happen in a spreadsheet if the current or active cell is B4 and you pressed enter key, ____________.

e. A pre-programmed formula is basically a ____________.

3. State whether the following statements are true (T) or false (F).

a. Copying refers to placing data from one place to another. ☐

b. Ctrl+A key combination is used to select a row. ☐

c. AutoFill is a feature to copy data simply by dragging the fill handle to the cells to be filled in. ☐

d. Fill Handle is a small black square that appears at the bottom right corner of the selected cell. It is used to auto fill list items, to fill custom lists, etc. ☐

e. You can edit the contents of a cell in the Formula bar. ☐

4. Give the steps for following.

a. To insert a column in a worksheet

b. To delete a row in a worksheet

c. To move data from one column to another.

d. To set a row height in a worksheet

e. To AutoFit column width

5. Answer the following questions in brief.

a. Which symbol is used to begin a formula in MS Excel?

b. What is the use of the AutoFill feature?

c. What is the function of the undo and redo commands?

d. Explain the method to insert multiple columns in a worksheet.

e. What are the rules of using formulas in Excel?

Experiential Learning

Lab Activities

1. Create a spreadsheet using MS Excel. The spreadsheet should contain information about the top 10 coding languages used today. The columns should be: S. No., Coding Language, Percentage of people using it today. Use the internet to get the correct information.

2. Anchal went to the mall and bought the following items.

Item	Number of items	Cost of each item (₹)	Total
Clothes	5	1500	
Shoes	2	3500	
Tennis racquet	1	2200	
Bedsheet	1	1500	
Total			

Create a sheet to find out the amount Anchal spent on each item and the total in the mall.

3. Open MS Excel and enter the data into your worksheet as given here:

Once completed, follow these instructions:

a. Add one more row with the name "Abhi Dash".

b. Change the First Name on row 4 to Nitin and that on Row 1 to Abhinav.

c. Add a new column to add the age of each individual.

d. By using the move option, move row 2 to row 5.

e. Insert a new column C (to the left of Age column) to add Middle names.

f. Save the worksheet as names.xlxs.

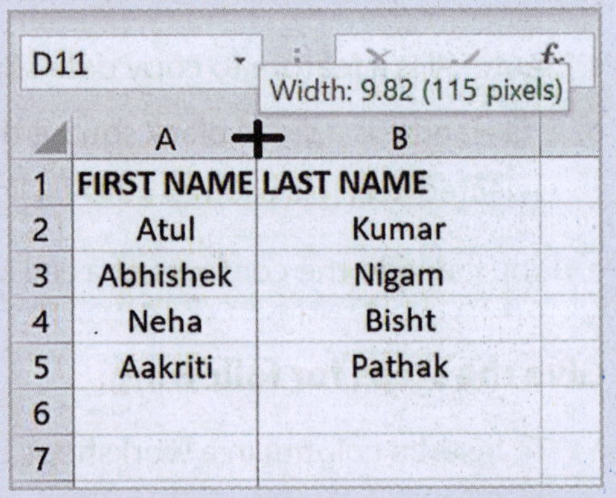

Collaboration

Group Activity

Waste segregation means dividing waste into dry and wet. When you segregate waste at home daily, you are winning half the battle as a responsible citizen. Form a group of 5 students to do a survey in your building/locality/family circle to find how many households segregate waste around us. Create an Excel sheet to add a minimum of 50 entries with their address and if they segregate waste. Towards the end, find the sum of households segregating waste.

Chapter

7

Database and DBMS—An Introduction

After reading this chapter, I will be able to:

- ✔ Define database and DBMS with real life examples.
- ✔ Design a database and describe different data types.
- ✔ Define a primary key and build query statements.
- ✔ Create a table, insert data, save and edit a table.
- ✔ Build query statements.

Brainstorm and explore!

On an online shopping website, such as Amazon, millions of people shop every day. Amazon has to remember what they shopped, whether they paid or not, the addresses to which products need to be sent, and even order history! How do you think Amazon manages all this data? Write your views here.

What is a Database?

A database is used to store information and manipulate them. The organization of a database is similar to that of a table in MS Excel and MS Word. Data is organized into rows and columns.

> A database is a systematic and organized collection of interrelated information of a specific type.

Structure of a Database

Every database has a specific structure. This structure allows users to effectively enter and access information, use other sets of data, and leverage the relational power among data enabled by MS Access. The components of a database are as follows:

- **Field**: Field is the first row in the database and it contains the indication of type of information in the column. A field contains key attributes in a record. For example, the staff ID column would contain the staff IDs of all teachers in a school.
- **Record**: A collection of all rows in a database can be taken as a record. An example of a record would be the attendance register of a class room that contains information about the roll number and attendance (Yes/No) data against dates for each student.

Fig. 7.1 | *Databases connected with each other*

Together, fields and records are stored in the form of a **table**.

The structure of a database in MS Access mimics structures in real life. For example, suppose your school wants to create a database of all students and teachers in class 10. Starting with the database name, it is advisable for all names to be easily recognizable. The database would be called ClassTen and would contain two records: Teacher and Students. Just as their real-world characteristics, the Teacher records would contain fields such as Staff ID and Name. The Students record would contain key student fields such as roll number. The structure of the ClassTen database would be as follows:

Database	ClassTen	
Records	Teacher	Students
Fields	Staff ID, Name, Subject	Roll No., Name

Forms, Queries and Reports are also structured forms of interacting with information in a database. A form allows users to enter data into tables. As the name suggests, a query enables users to ask questions in a particular format on a database. Reports are used to summarise data from tables and/or queries in a printable format.

Database Management System

A Database Management System (DBMS) is an application software that allows users to create, store, modify, extract and view a database as per their requirements.

Advantages of DBMS

Some of the advantages of DBMS are as follows:

- **Sharing of data**: Multiple users can work on the same database.

- **Secure**: To prevent deletions or unintended modifications, data can be protected in a database.
- **Access control**: The administrator has complete control over the database. Hence, the data access can be granted to selected authorized people, based on their need.
- **Consistency**: If multiple people are using the same database at once, they can access it without any glitches.
- **Redundancy**: Redundancy means the duplication of data. MS Access makes sure that multiple copies of the same data need not be maintained across a database.
- **Data integrity**: Data integrity allows users to preemptively ensure that the data is stored in a particular format and acceptable values can only be entered. For example, the field called Roll No. will only accept numerical values.

Microsoft Access

Microsoft Access is a Relational Database Management System (RDBMS) of the MS Office Suite that organizes data in the form of tables. It creates a relationship among tables on the basis of the common fields. Data can be entered, updated, deleted, viewed and retrieved with the help of the tools present in MS Access.

Components of the MS Access Window

The various components of MS Access are as follows:

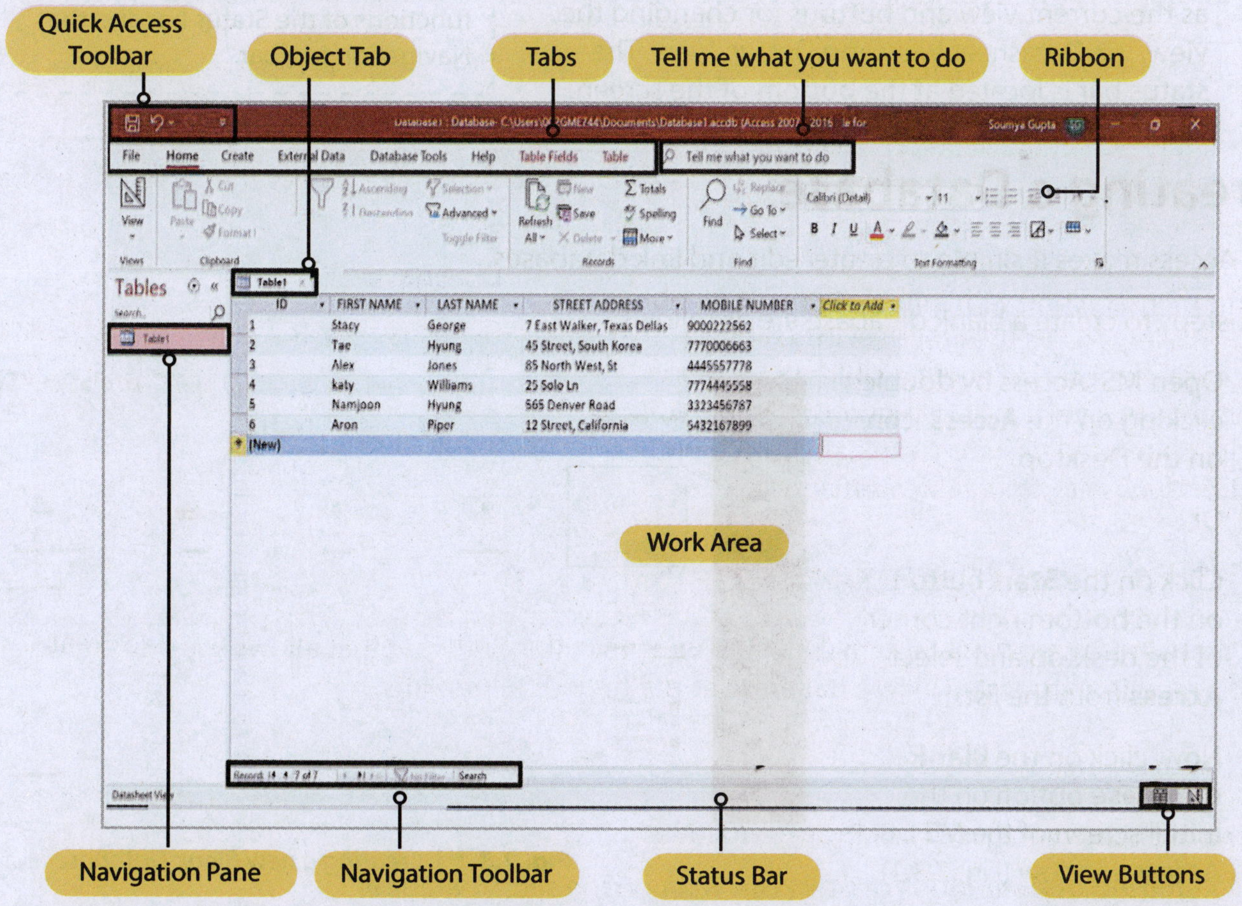

Fig. 7.2 | *Parts of MS Access window*

- **Title Bar**: This is the top most bar of the window that displays the name of the file and the Minimize, Maximize/Restore and Close options.
- **Quick Access Toolbar**: This toolbar is present on the top-left corner of the MS Access window. As the name suggests, it contains the most frequently used commands such as Save, Undo and Redo.
- **Ribbon**: It has the several sets of commands grouped together as tabs. Contextual tabs are the tabs that selectively appear when certain objects are used.
- **Tell Me What You Want To Do**: It acts as a quickly accessible help desk of commands and information to use MS Access.
- **Navigation Pane**: This pane is present on the left side of the MS Access window. It shows the name of all the objects in a database such as Tables, Queries, Forms, Reports, etc.
- **Navigation Toolbar**: Navigation toolbar enables users to navigate through objects. It contains information such as the current record number, search bar, etc.
- **Work Area**: As the names suggests, users can work on the tables, objects, and records in the work area.
- **Object Tab**: This tab describes the contents of the work area.
- **Status Bar**: Status bar contains information such as the current view and buttons for changing the view, viz. Datasheet View and Design View. The status bar is located at the bottom of the screen.

Clear up!

Explore MS Access in the school computer lab and make a list of all functions of the Status bar and the Navigation toolbar.

Creating a Database

MS Access makes it simple to create, edit and link databases.

The steps to create a blank database are as follows:

1. Open MS Access by double clicking on the **Access** icon on the Desktop.

   Or

   Click on the **Start** button on the bottom right corner of the desktop and select **Access** from the list.

2. Now, click on the **Blank database** option on the initial screen of the MS Access window (Fig. 7.3.1).

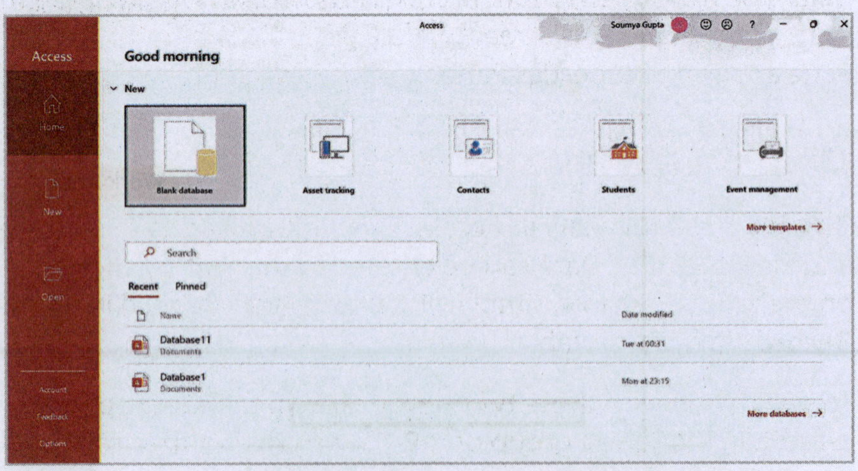

Fig. 7.3.1 | *Creating a new Blank Database*

3. Specify the file name in the **File Name** text box. Here, you can also change the location of your file by clicking on the folder icon placed next to the **File Name** text box. Click on the **Create** button (Fig. 7.3.2).

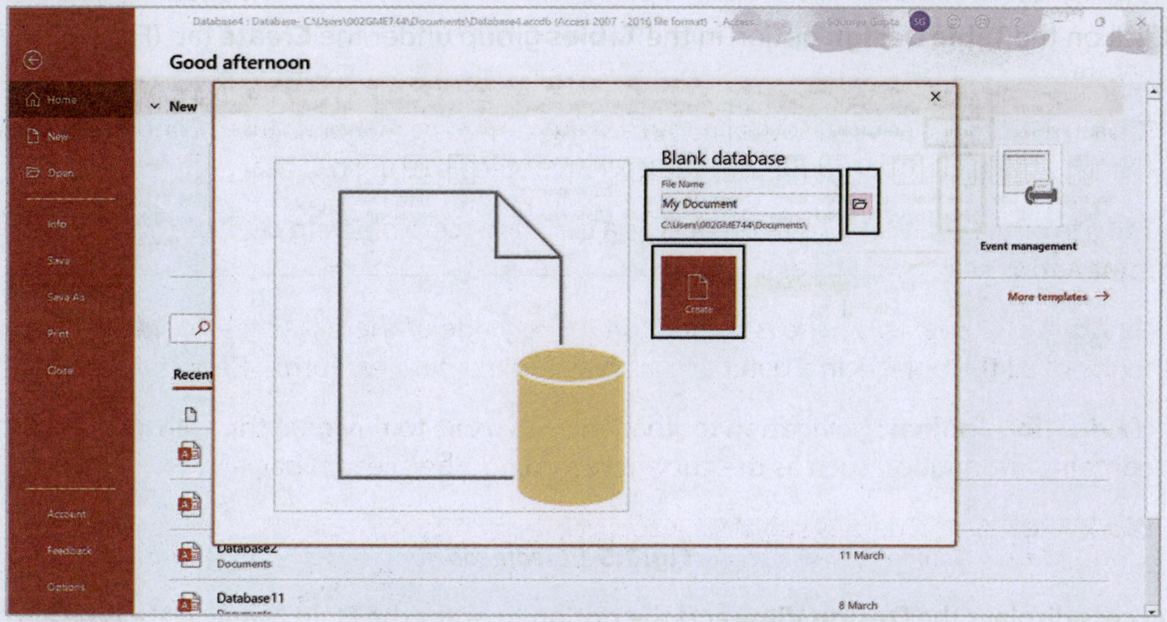

Fig. 7.3.2 | *Specifying the file name*

A new database will be created with the default blank table named as **Table1**.

Views of a Table

We can see the database in two views as discussed below:

Design View

This view is used to add field names, their data types and description. There are two parts of the Data view screen: Field Grid Pane and Field Properties Pane.

Datasheet View

This is the default view in Access. This view is used to enter and view the data. Data can be entered in the cells by clicking on them. To add a row, simply click on the **New Record** in the **Record Navigation** tab.

To switch between these two views, click on the **View** option present in the **Views** group on the Home tab and then select the desired view.

Clear up!

There is one more way to switch between these two views. Explore MS Access views in the school computer lab and note down your observation.

[**Hint:** *Bottom-right corner of the MS Access window*]

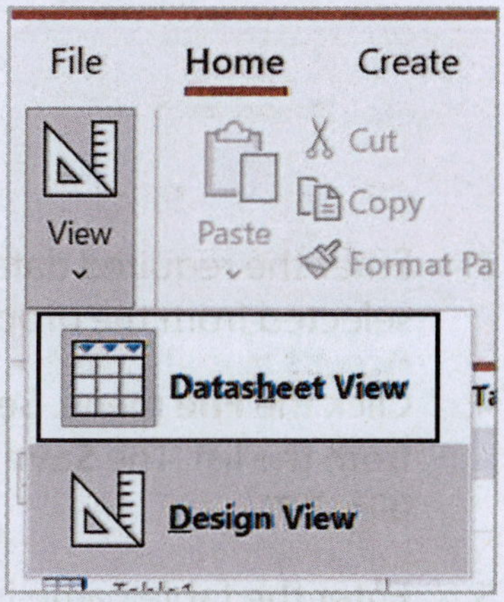

Fig. 7.4 | *View group*

Creating and Saving a Table

The steps to create a table in the Design View are as follows:

1. Click on the **Table Design** option in the **Tables** group under the **Create** tab (Fig. 7.5).

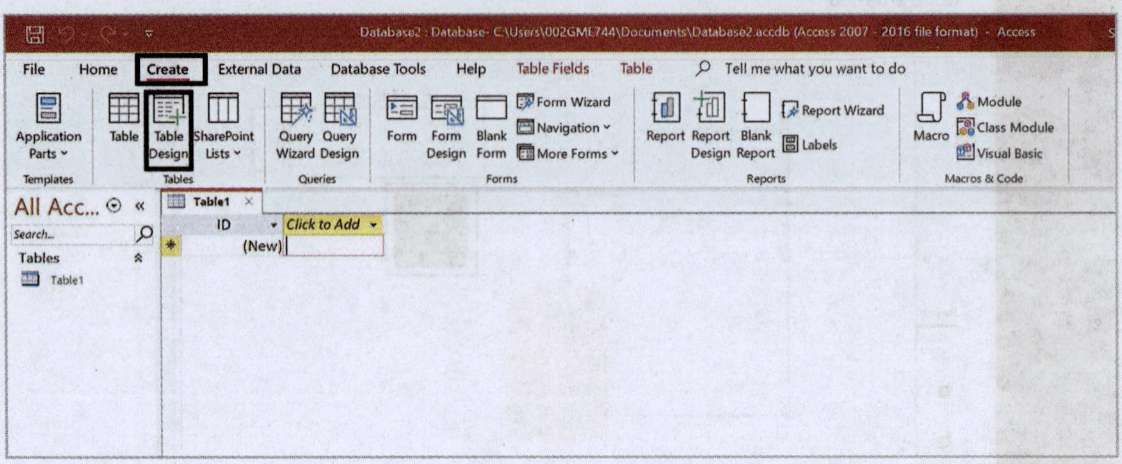

Fig. 7.5 | *Create tab*

2. Access displays the **Design View** and the option to enter the Field Name, Data Type and Description (Fig. 7.6).

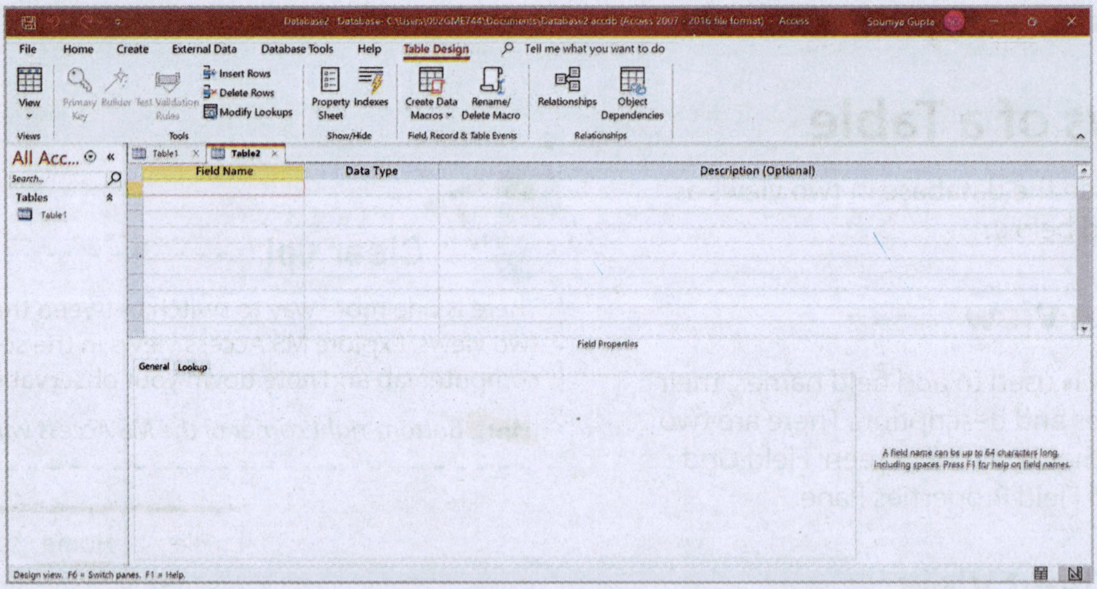

Fig. 7.6 | *Table opens in the Design View*

3. Enter the required data. Data Type can be selected from the drop-down options.

4. Click the **File** menu. Select the **Save** option from the list. The **Save As** dialog box appears (Fig. 7.7).

5. Enter the table name in the **Table Name** text box. Click **OK**.

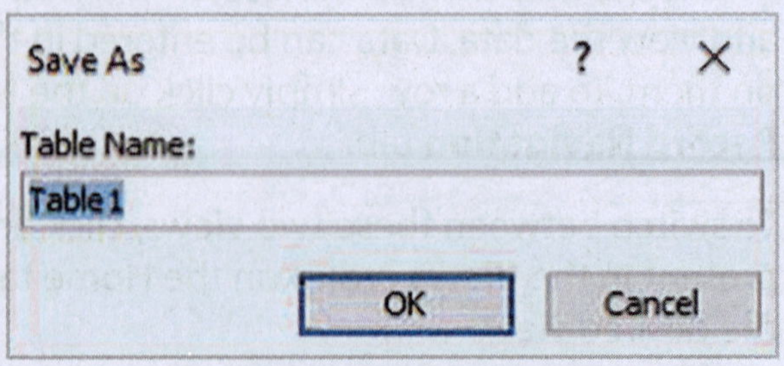

Fig. 7.7 | *Saving a table*

Entering Data in a Table

The next step after defining the table structure is to add field names to the table. To add the field names, follow the steps given here:

1. Click the table where the data has to be entered.
2. On the **HOME** tab, in the **Views** group, click on the **View** drop-down menu (Fig. 7.8).

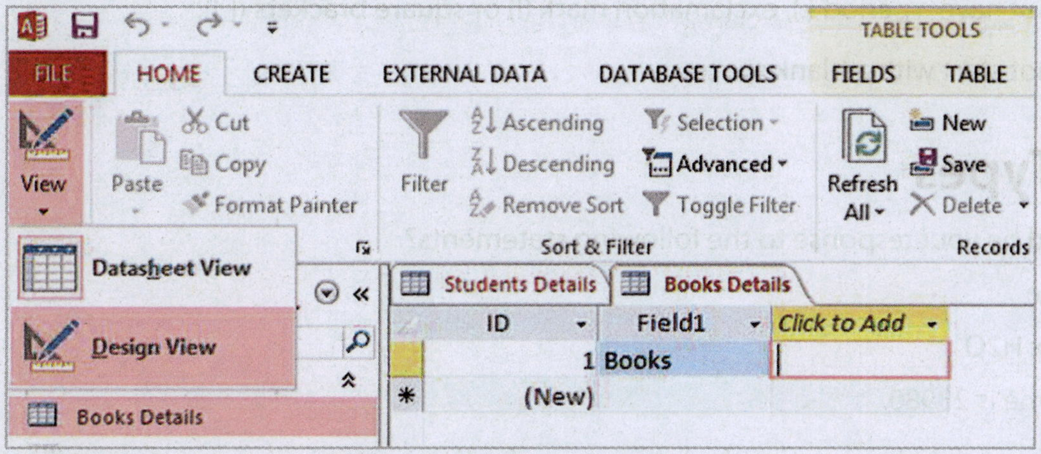

Fig. 7.8 | *Entering data into a table*

3. Select **Design View** option from the drop-down menu. The table opens in the **Design View** (Fig. 7.9).

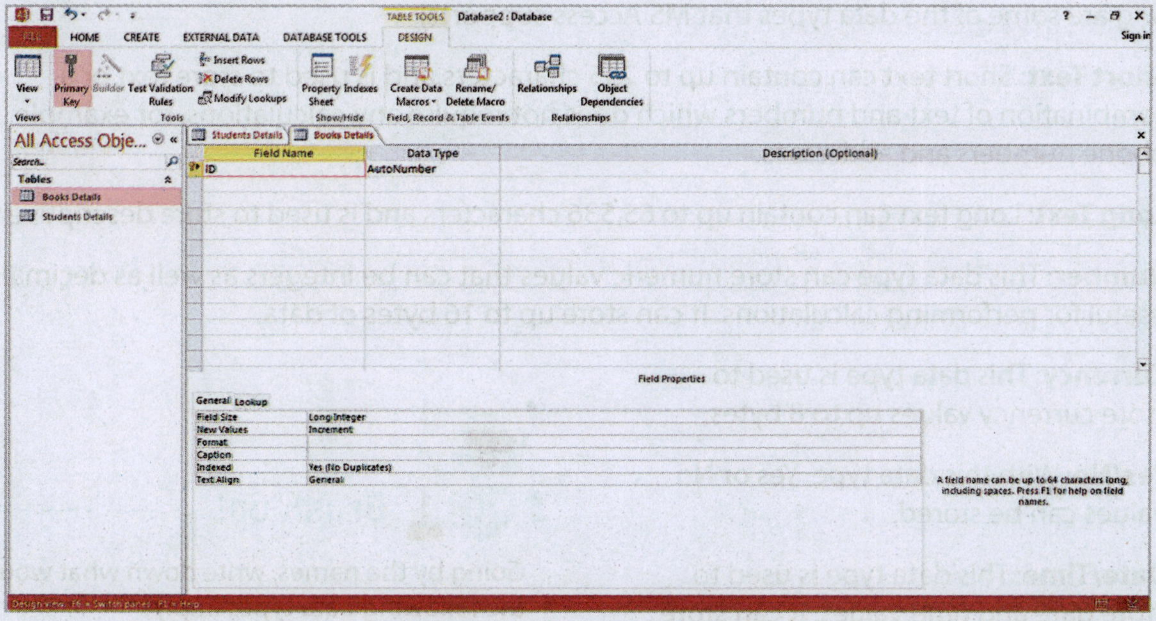

Fig. 7.9 | *The table in Design View*

4. Enter field names.
5. Press the **Tab** key to move to the **Data Type** column.
6. Click the drop-down arrow in the **Data Type** column and select a data type.
7. Similarly, enter other field names and their data types.

Rules for Naming a Field

The following rules should be followed while naming a field in a table.

1. The field name should not be more than 64 characters.
2. The field name can include lowercase, uppercase or mixed case letters, numbers and an underscore.
3. It cannot have a period (.), exclamation mark (!) or square brackets ([ ]).
4. It cannot start with a blank space.

Data Types

What would be your response to the following statements?

1. 2 + tree
2. water x H2O
3. My name is 23980.

While humans might have out-of-the box answers for these questions, a computer will return an error. Computer cannot understand and process all these instructions. Data types are useful here because they allow computers to process data in a standard form. For example, a field whose data type is 'Number' can only store the numeric data. The text data is not allowed here.

Following are some of the data types that MS Access supports:

- **Short Text**: Short text can contain up to 255 characters and is used to store text or a combination of text and numbers which does not require any calculations, for example, phone numbers and addresses.
- **Long Text**: Long text can contain up to 65,536 characters and is used to store descriptive fields.
- **Number**: This data type can store numeric values that can be integers as well as decimals. It is useful for performing calculations. It can store up to 16 bytes of data.
- **Currency**: This data type is used to store currency values up to 8 bytes.
- **Yes/No**: With this data type, Yes or No values can be stored.
- **Date/Time**: This data type is used to store date and time values. It can store up to 8 bytes of data.
- **Calculated Field**: This data type is used to store value that need to be manipulated across queries, forms and tables.

Brush up!

Going by the names, write down what would the following data types imply?

- Hyperlink ____________
- AutoNumber ____________
- Attachment ____________

- **Lookup & Relationship**: This data type is used to store values that are searched in another table, query, or set of values. By default, the Number data type is assigned to the Lookup field.
- **OLE Object**: OLE Object is used to store data imported from another application such as MS Word, MS Excel, MS PowerPoint, etc.

Primary Key

Look at the following questions and write their answers.

Que 1. What is a unique feature of every member in your family?

Ans: Their names!

Que 2. What is a unique feature of every student in your class?

Ans: ______________________________

Que 3. What is a unique feature of every teacher in your school?

Ans: ______________________________

If we created a table named 'Family', the 'Name' field would be the unique feature since members in a family do not have the same names. The field Name in the table Family would be a Primary Key. Database uses the Primary Key field to set a unique value for each record in a table. This field cannot be left blank and a table can have only one Primary Key.

Specifying a Primary Key Field

To specify a Primary Key field, the steps are as follows:

1. Open the table in the **Design View** (Fig. 7.10).

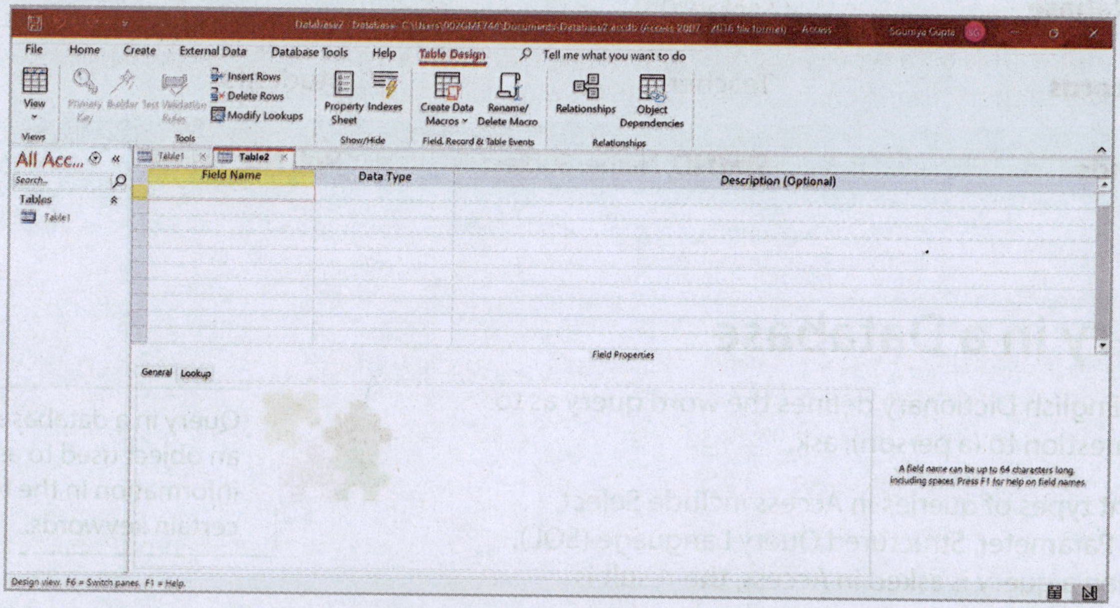

Fig. 7.10 | *Design View of a table*

2. Click on the **Primary Key** button present under the **Tools** group on the **Table Tools** tab.

Or

Right-click on the field that has to be set as the Primary Key. Click on the **Primary Key** option (Fig. 7.11).

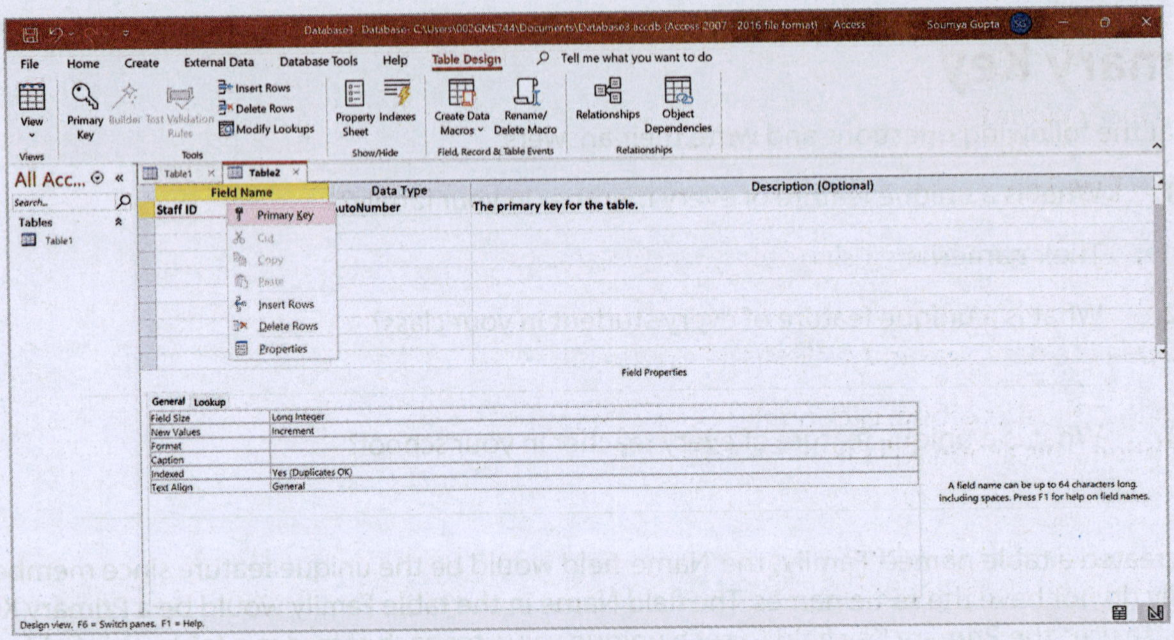

Fig. 7.11 | *Specifying the Primary Key option*

3. The Primary Key will be indicated with a small yellow lock. Save the changes in the table.

In the following records, the Primary Keys are marked in **bold**.

Database	Classroom	
Records	Teacher	Students
Fields	**Staff ID**, Name, Subject	**Roll No.**, Name

Query in a Database

Collins English Dictionary defines the word query as to put a question to (a person); ask.

Different types of queries in Access include Select, Action, Parameter, Structured Query Language (SQL), etc. When a query is asked in Access, the result is

Query in a database is an object used to ask information in the form of certain keywords.

returned in the form of a table. A query may involve a single table or multiple tables. Queries are used not only to summarize specific information but also to edit and analyze data.

Creating a Query

MS Access allows query creation in two ways:

- Query Design
- Query Wizard

Query Design

The steps to create a query using Query Design are as follows:

1. Open the database and click on the **Create** tab.
2. In the **Queries** group, click on the **Query Design** option. This action will open the **Add Table** dialog box (Fig. 7.12).
3. Select the table or tables where the query needs to be run and click on the **Add** button.
4. The **Query Design** view opens (Fig. 7.13). The top pane shows the table or tables selected for the query and the bottom pane shows the design grid (Fig. 7.14).

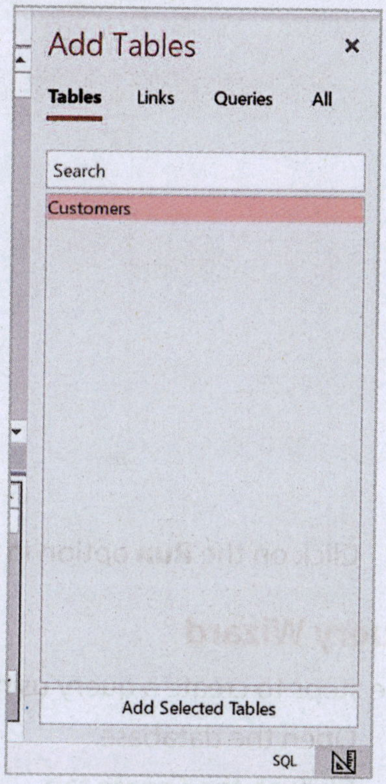

Fig. 7.12 | *Add Table dialog box*

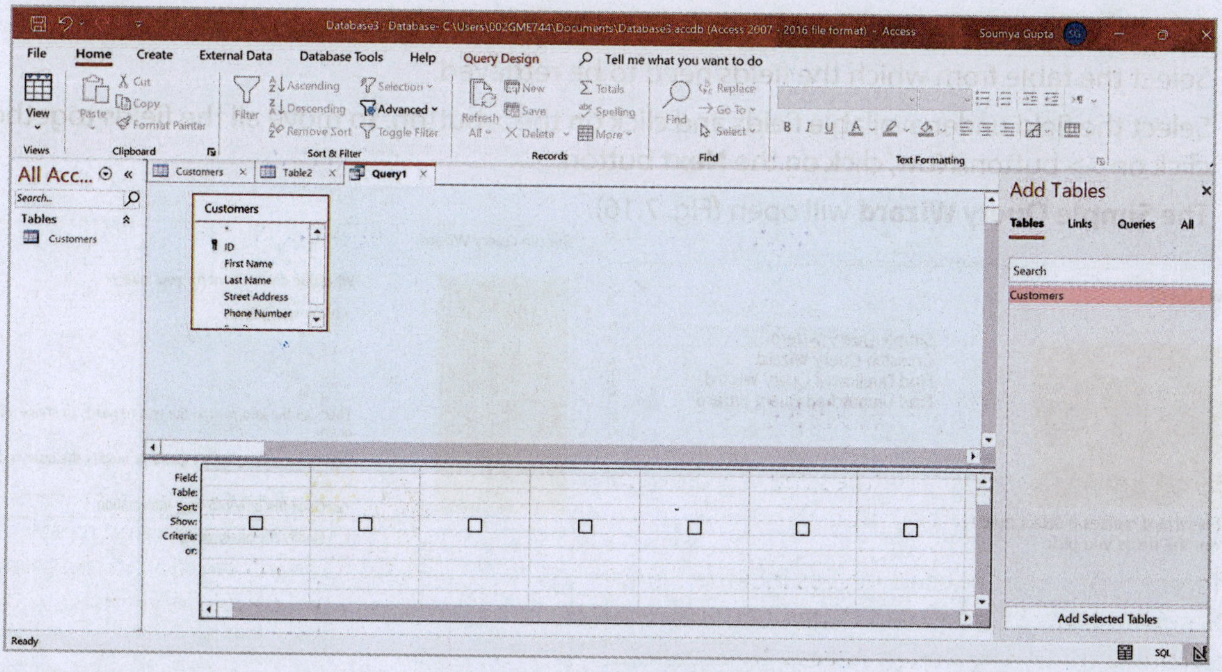

Fig. 7.13 | *Query Design view*

5. Navigate to the field that needs to be seen on the query table and double-click on it. This will insert the field in the bottom pane. Repeat the action with other fields and set the criteria by clicking on the data in **Criteria** option.

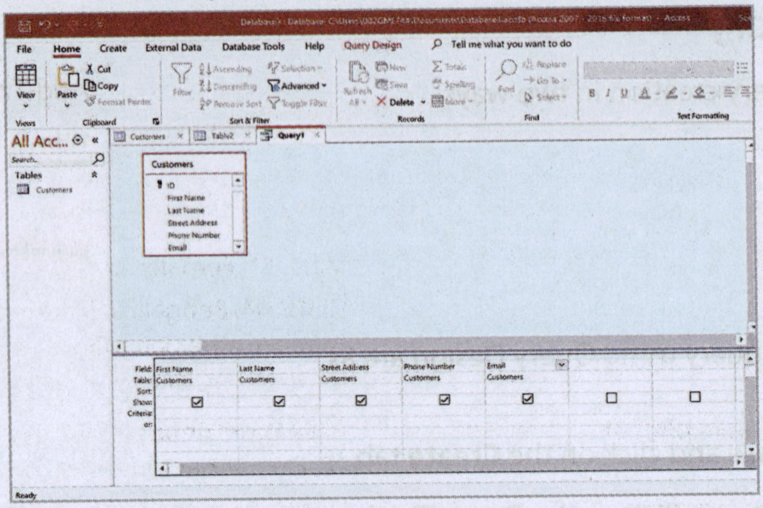

Fig. 7.14 | *Design Grid*

6. Click on the **Run** option in the **Results** group on the **Design** tab to execute the query.

Query Wizard

The steps to create a query using Query Wizard are as follows:

1. Open the database.
2. Click on the **Create** tab.
3. In the **Queries** group, click on the **Query Wizard**. This action will open the **New Query** dialog box (Fig. 7.15).
4. Select the **Simple Query Wizard** and click on the **OK** button.
5. Select the table from which the fields need to be retrieved.
6. Select the field under available fields and click on the > button. To move all the fields together, click on >> button. Now, click on the **Next** button.
7. The **Simple Query Wizard** will open (Fig. 7.16).

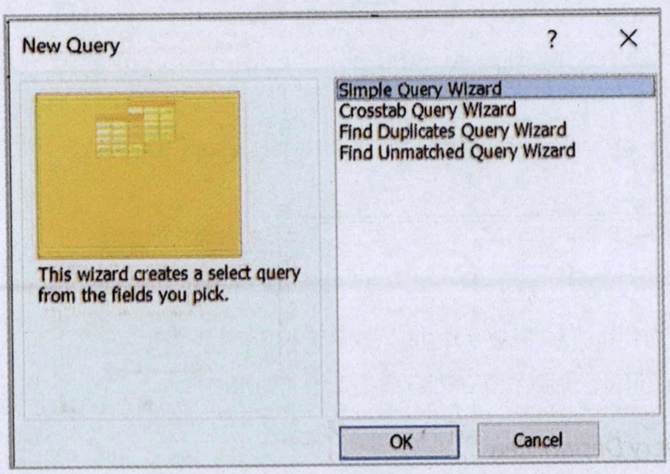

Fig. 7.15 | *New Query dialog box*

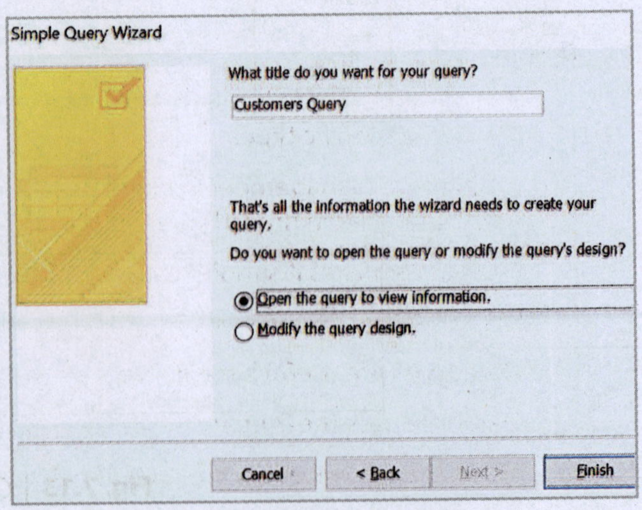

Fig. 7.16 | *Simple Query Wizard*

8. In this step, give a name to the query and click on the **Finish** button.

Link up!

As humans, we find it difficult to intuitively grasp very large numbers. For example, the population of India is 1,369,000,000!

To simplify this, let us consider that India is made up of only 100 people. Now, it is easy-to-classify this small data as follows:

Gender ratio	Male: 51, Female: 49
Language	Hindi: 44, Bengali: 8, Marathi: 7, Telugu: 7, Tamil: 6, other languages : 28
Age	0–19: 41, 20–59: 50, Above 60: 9
Access to mobile phones	Have basic phones: 35, Have smart phones: 26, Do not have phones: 39
Access to the internet	Do not have the internet access: 60, Have the internet access: 40
Access to clean drinking water	Do not have access to clean drinking water: 53, Have access to clean drinking water: 47

Clear up!

In the previous classes, we have learned about other MS Office applications such as MS Word, MS Excel and MS Power Point. Since MS Access has a similar layout, write down the steps for carrying out the following in MS Access:

- Save
- Close
- Exit

Today I learned!

- A database is a systematic and organized collection of interrelated information of a specific type.
- A Database Management System (DBMS) is an application software that allows users to work with databases in myriad ways.
- MS Access makes it simple to create, edit and link databases.
- MS Access has two views: Design view and Database view.
- Data types are useful because they allow computers to process data in a standard form.
- Database uses the Primary Key field to set a unique value to each record in a table.
- MS Access allows query creation in two ways: Query Design and Query Wizard.

Revise and polish!

Learning Skills

1. Tick (✔) the correct answer.

a. DBMS stands for:

(i) Data management software ☐ (ii) Database modification system ☐

(iii) Database management system ☐ (iv) Database memory system ☐

b. What is the first row in a database that indicates the type of information in the column called?

(i) Field ☐ (ii) Row ☐

(iii) Column ☐ (iv) Cell ☐

c. In which of the following views, a database can be viewed in MS Access?

(i) Database view ☐ (ii) Design view ☐

(iii) All of the above ☐ (iv) Display view ☐

d. Which of the following tabs describes the contents of the work area?

(i) Object tab ☐ (ii) Layout tab ☐

(iii) Design tab ☐ (iv) Insert tab ☐

e. Which of the following data types stores currency values?

(i) Date ☐ (ii) Short Text ☐

(iii) Currency ☐ (iv) String ☐

f. How many characters can be contained in Short text?

(i) 254 ☐ (ii) 255 ☐

(iii) 256 ☐ (iv) 230 ☐

g. Which of the following in a database is an object used to ask information in the form of certain keywords?

(i) Query ☐ (ii) Quiz ☐

(iii) Inquiry ☐ (iv) Quote ☐

h. In which form, the result is returned when a query is asked in MS Access?

(i) Table ☐ (ii) Long Text ☐

(iii) Short Text ☐ (iv) Column ☐

i. How is a Primary Key indicated with?

(i) Yellow Lock ☐ (ii) Green Lock ☐

(iii) Blue Lock ☐ (iv) White Lock ☐

j. What is the other way of query creation in MS Access, if the first way is Query Design?

(i) Query Layout ☐ (ii) Datasheet View ☐

(iii) Query Wizard ☐ (iv) Query Design ☐

2. Fill in the blanks.

file record query DBMS database

a. A ________________ is used to store information and manipulate them.

b. A ________________ is an application software that allows user to create, store, modify, extract and view a database as per their requirements.

c. A collection of all the rows in a database is called a ________________.

d. A collection of records is called a ________________.

e. A ________________ is a question to the database.

3. Match the following.

a.	Short Text	(i)	Up to 8 bytes
b.	Numbers	(ii)	File
c.	Date/Time	(iii)	Decimals and integers
d.	Attachment	(iv)	Up to 255 characters
e.	Currency	(v)	22/02/2022

4. State whether the following statements are true (T) or false (F).

a. A collection of all the rows in a database can be taken as a records. ☐

b. MS Access is a system software. ☐

c. There are three views in MS Access. ☐

d. The Currency data type is used to store currency values up to 8 bytes. ☐

e. Queries can be create using the Create tab. ☐

5. Answer the following questions.

a. Write a short note on database and their applications.

b. Write the steps to create a database in MS Access.

c. Describe any four data types in MS Access.

d. What are the different ways of creating a query on MS Access? Write their name.

e. Write a note on the views in MS Access.

6. **Identify the Primary key in the following records.**

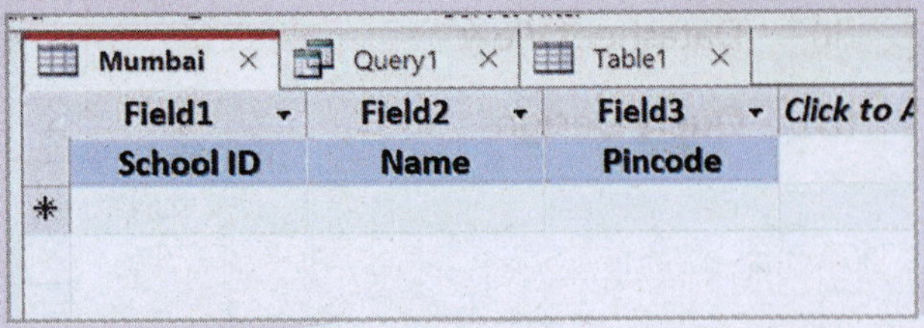

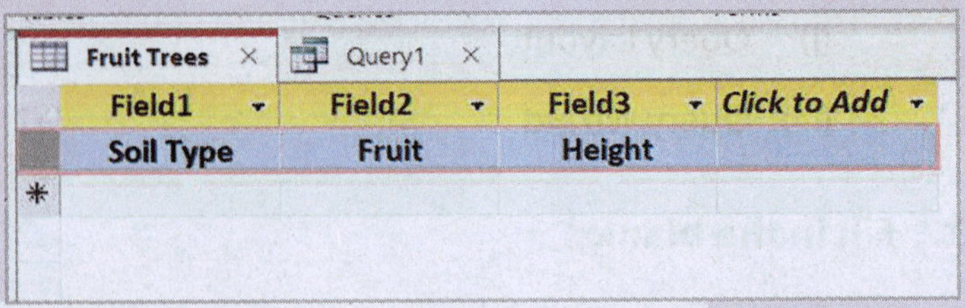

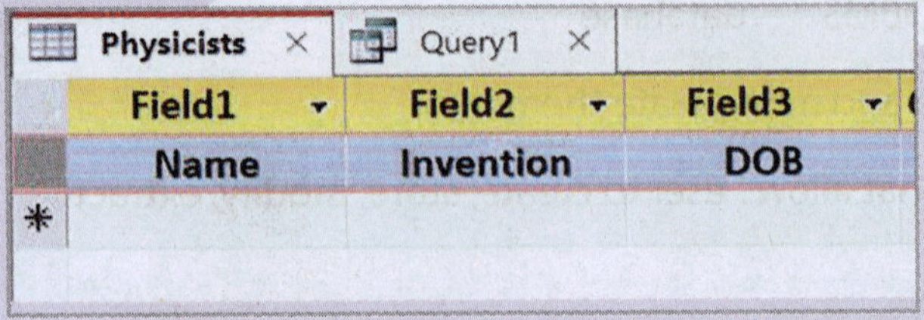

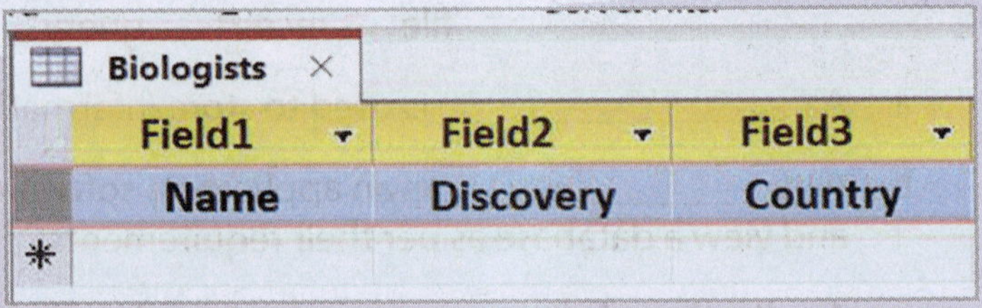

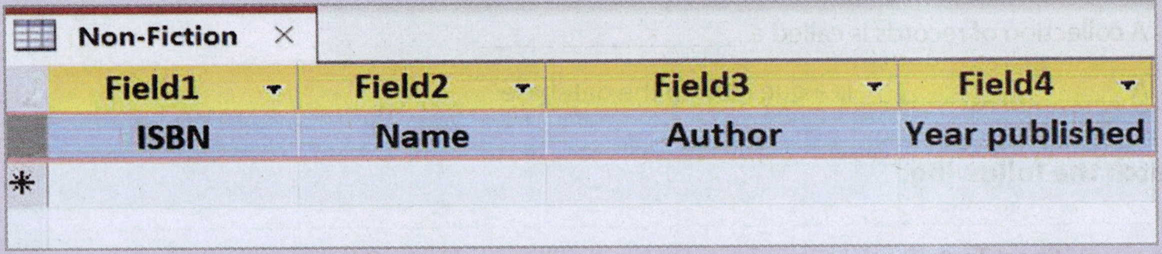

Database	Records	Fields
Schools in Metro Cities	Mumbai	School ID, Name, Pincode
Trees of India	Fruit Trees	Soil Type, Fruit, Height
Prominent Scientists	Physicists	Name, Invention, DOB
	Biologists	Name, Discovery, Country
Books	Non-Fiction	ISBN, Name, Author, Year published

Lab Activities

1. Create the following database in MS Access with three records, three fields and five rows populated within each record. Mark the primary key and set a default value in one of the fields, if applicable.
   a. Types of computers
   b. Widely used apps today
   c. The greatest sports persons
2. Create the following database in MS Access with two records, three fields and three rows populated. Now, discuss with your classmates about the database and understand if the fields are similar, why they choose their respective fields and records, and how they have organized their information. Explain your thought process to your classmates as well.
   a. Fun board games
   b. Your favourite cartoon characters

Chapter

8

More on HTML

After reading this chapter, I will be able to:

- ✔ Explain and create different types of lists.
- ✔ Describe how to insert a table in a web page.
- ✔ Describe how to insert audio and video tags.

Brainstorm and explore!

HTML is the markup language used to create websites. Write down the functions of each tag.

1. `<i>`

   ____

2. `<sub>`

   ____

3. `<sup>`

   ____

4. `<img>`

   ____

5. `<br>`

   ____

6. `<a>`

   ____

We have studied about HTML in the previous class and used various tags and elements to create a web page.

In this chapter, we will learn some more features of HTML, such as creating lists and tables and embedding images, audios and videos.

Lists

Lists are used to present data in a neat and organized manner. A list is a record of a series of items, usually arranged according to a system. We can also display lists on a web page using HTML list elements. In HTML, lists can be of four types:

1. Ordered lists
2. Unordered lists
3. Description lists
4. Nested lists

Ordered List

An **ordered list** is a collection of items in a particular sequence. This list is represented by the <ol> tag in HTML. Each list item starts with the <li> tag. It is used when the sequence of the steps is important.

Syntax:

```
<ol> #Start of an ordered list
    <li>list items</li>
    <li>list items</li>
</ol>
```

For example, when writing a recipe or an algorithm, a numbered ordered list is used (Fig. 8.1).

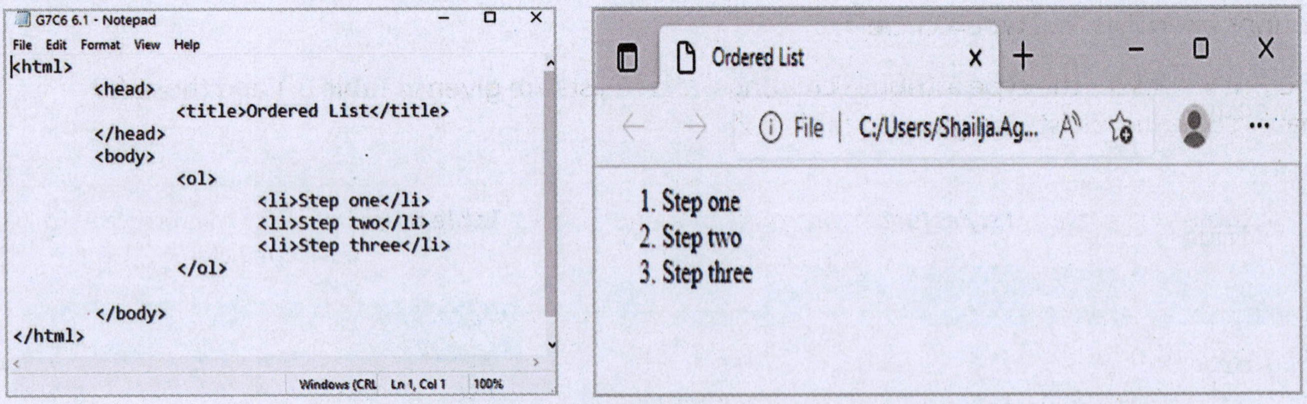

Fig. 8.1 | *Ordered list*

Unordered List

An **unordered list** is a collection of items that do not require to be displayed in any specific order. For example, a list of fruits available in the market. This list is represented by the <ul> tag in HTML. This tag replaces numbers with bullets.

Syntax:

```
<ul> #Start of an unordered list
    <li>list items</li>
    <li>list items</li>
</ul>
```

For example, when creating a list of fruits, the unordered list is used (Fig. 8.2).

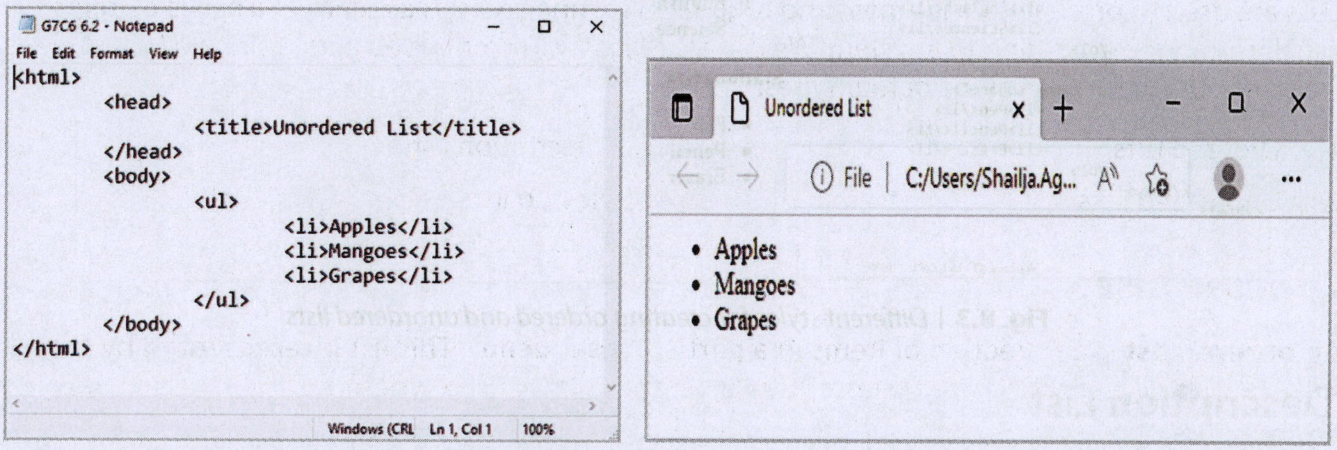

Fig. 8.2 | *Unordered list*

Changing the Styles of Lists

The default style for an ordered list is numbers (1., 2., 3., …) and for an unordered list is bullets (•). We can change these styles by using a common attribute called **type** and the corresponding value.

Syntax:

For ordered lists: <ol type="a">

For unordered lists: <ul type="circle">

Different values for the type attribute creating ordered lists are given in Table 8.1 and those for creating unordered lists are given in Table 8.2.

Table 8.1 | *Different styles for creating ordered lists*

Type	Description	Example
1	Numbers	1, 2, 3, 4, ...
A	Uppercase letters	A, B, C, D, ...
a	Lowercase letters	a, b, c, d, ...
I	Uppercase Roman numbers	I, II, III, IV, ...
i	Lowercase Roman numbers	i, ii, iii, iv, ...

Table 8.2 | *Different styles for creating unordered lists*

Type	Description	Example
disc	Bullet symbol	•
circle	Hollow bullet	o
square	Filled square	♦
none	No symbol	

For example, refer to the HTML program given in Fig. 8.3 and the corresponding output, showing both ordered and unordered lists with different bullet styles.

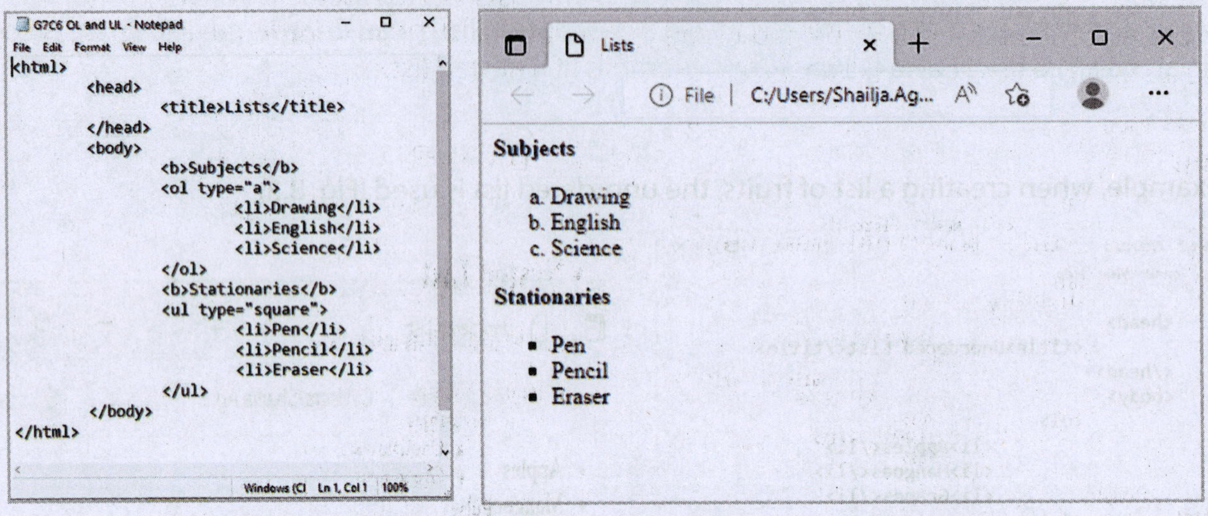

Fig. 8.3 | *Different styles for creating ordered and unordered lists*

Description List

A **description list** is used when we need to describe each list in detail. It is a list of terms followed by their descriptions. A description list is also called **definition list**.

The <dl> tag defines the description list. It is used along with the <dt> tag (definition term) that defines the term, and the <dd> tag (definition description) describes each term.

Syntax:

```
<dl> #Start of a description list
    <dt>Heading</dt>
    <dd> Subheading</dd>
  <dd> Subheading</dd>
</dl>
```

For example, when creating a list of various food items, a description list is used (Fig. 8.4).

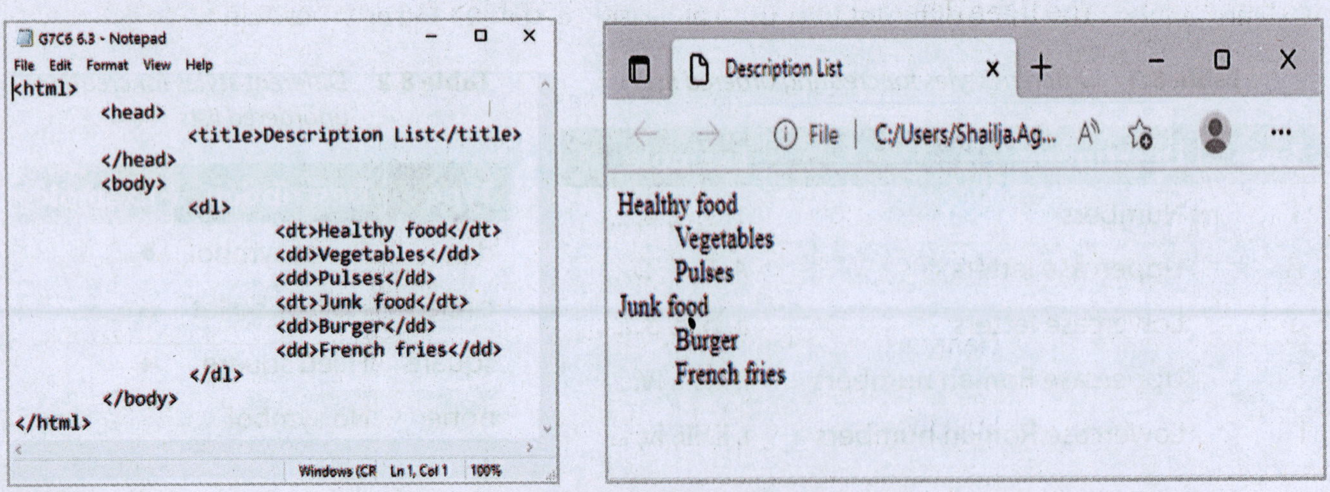

Fig. 8.4 | *Description list*

Nested Lists

Like nested loops, lists can also be nested, that is, these lists can be used inside other lists. For example, an ordered list can be nested inside a description list, or an unordered list can be placed inside an ordered list. Figure 8.5 shows an example of a nested list.

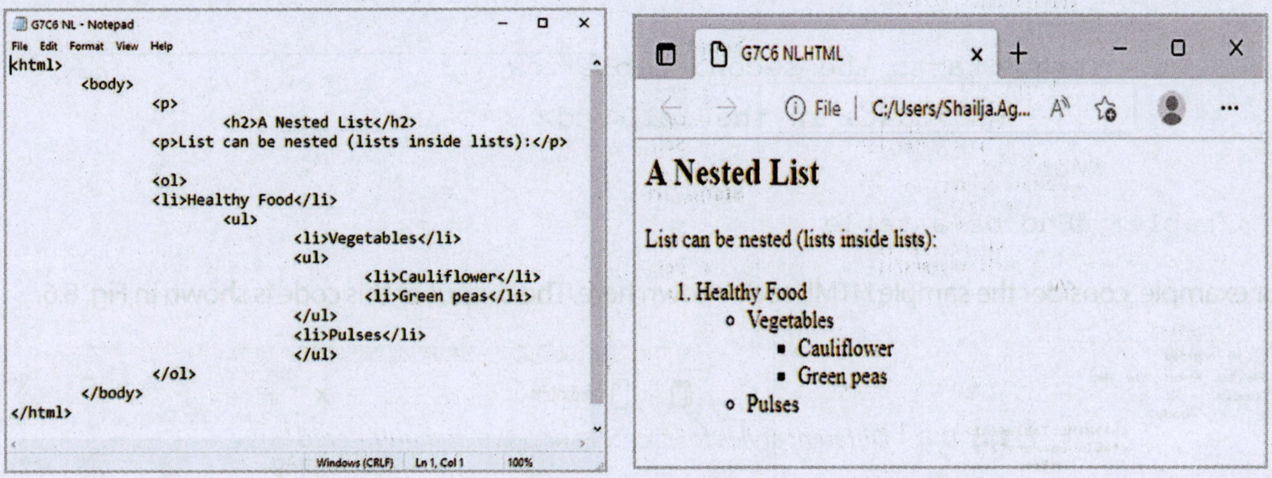

Fig. 8.5 | *Nested list*

Brush up!

Write an HTML program to display five names of IT personalities. Which list style will you use for this?

____

____

Table Tag

Other than images, links and lists, another important element used on a website is a table. Tables are used for comparisons, or simply to make a website look more structured. HTML uses the <table> tag to define a table. The three different tags used alongside a <table> tag are shown in Table 8.3.

Table 8.3 | *Tags used in the <table> tag*

Tag	Description
<tr>	Specifies the table row.
<tr>	Defines the table header.
<td>	Specifies the data inside a cell.

Syntax:

```
<table> #Start of a table
        <tr> # Starts the first table row
                <td> data in the cell</td>
        </tr>
        <tr> #Starts the second table row
                <td> data in the cell</td>
        </tr>
</table> #End of a table
```

For example, consider the sample HTML code shown here. The output of this code is shown in Fig. 8.6.

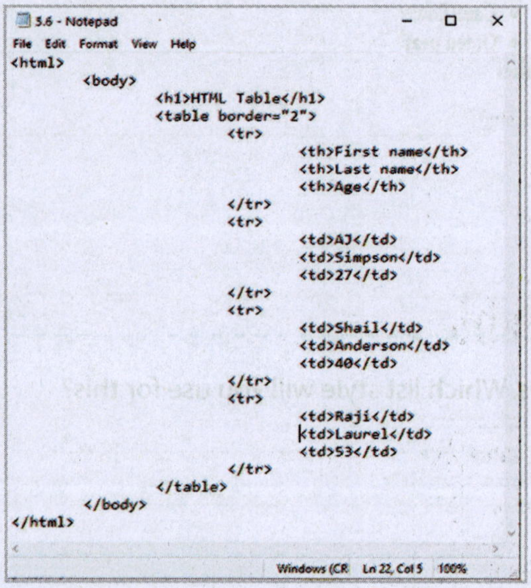

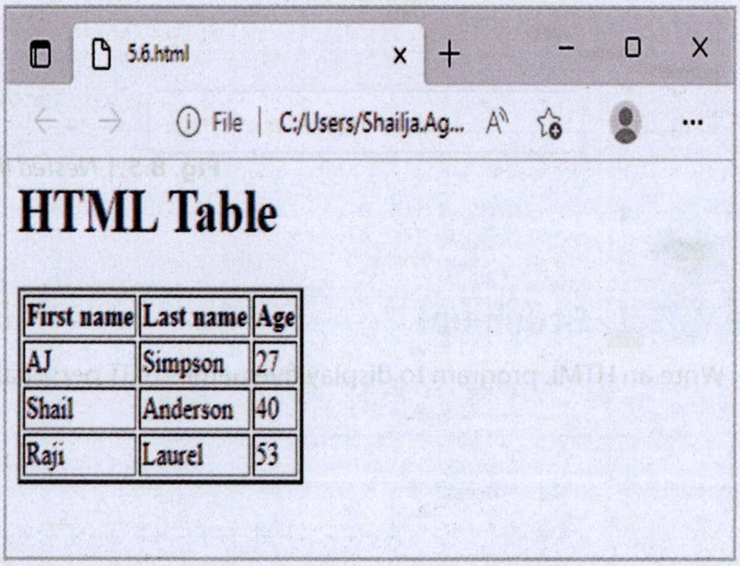

Fig. 8.6 | *Table in HTML*

Soak up!

By default, a table has no border in HTML. Some of the attributes for <table> tag, such as border, height and width, are not supported by HTML5. These attributes have been incorporated in CSS or Cascading Style Sheet. A CSS can be defined as a computer language, which is used along with HTML, for creating websites.

Clear up!

Create your report card using HTML. The report card should have two columns, 'Subject' and 'Grades/Marks'.

Colspan

Colspan is an attribute of the <td> tag. It is used to make a cell span more than one column.

Syntax:

```
<td colspan="number"> ;number= number of columns that will be merged
```

If we need to find the sum of the ages of all three entries that would require only two columns, which would mean that the first two columns will have to be merged. This is made possible using the colspan attribute. The code shown in Fig. 8.7 shows how to use this attribute. A new row 'Total' will be added to the code given in Fig. 8.6.

span: the amount of space that something covers

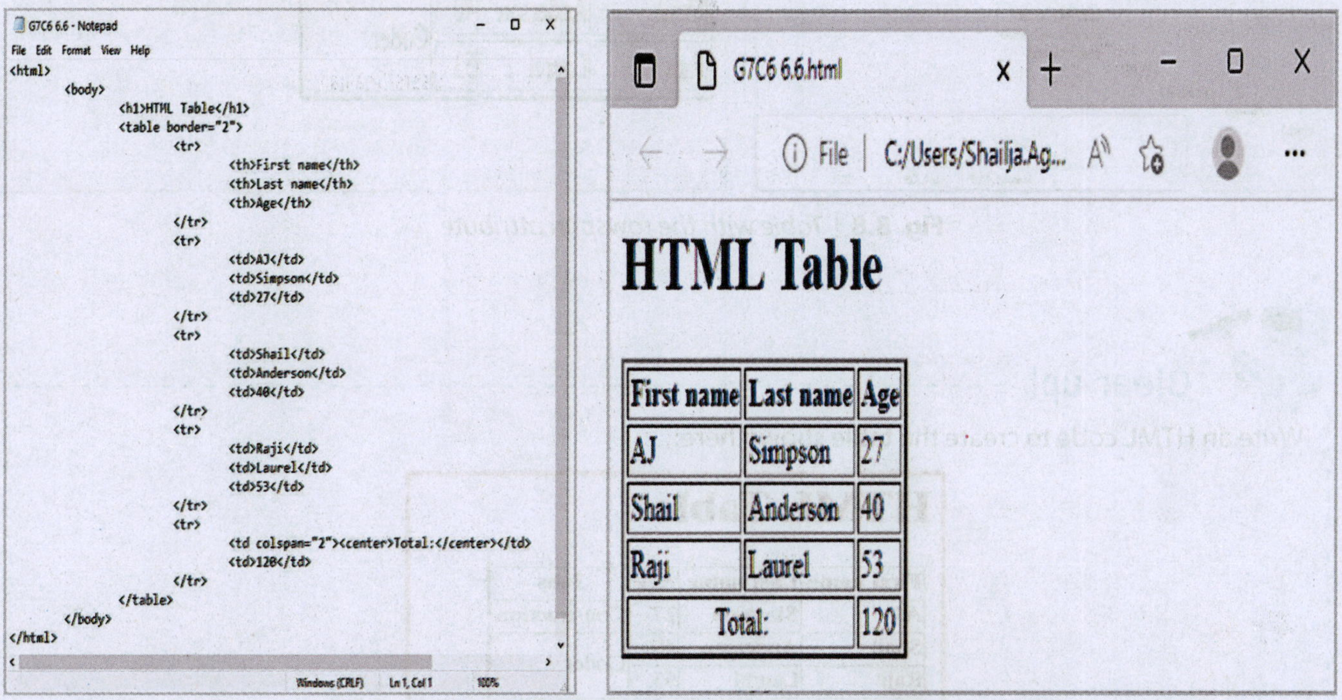

Fig. 8.7 | *Table with the colspan attribute*

Rowspan

As the colspan attribute is used for columns, the attribute rowspan is used with the <td> tag to merge two or more rows.

Syntax:

```
<td rowspan="number"> ;number= number of rows that will be merged
```

For example, let us say we want to insert a fourth column named Jobs to the table given in Fig. 8.6. Here, Shail and Raji both work as coders, whereas AJ is into the construction business. In this case, we need to merge the third and fourth rows using the rowspan attribute, thus, giving us a table cell that spans 2 rows, as shown in Fig. 8.8.

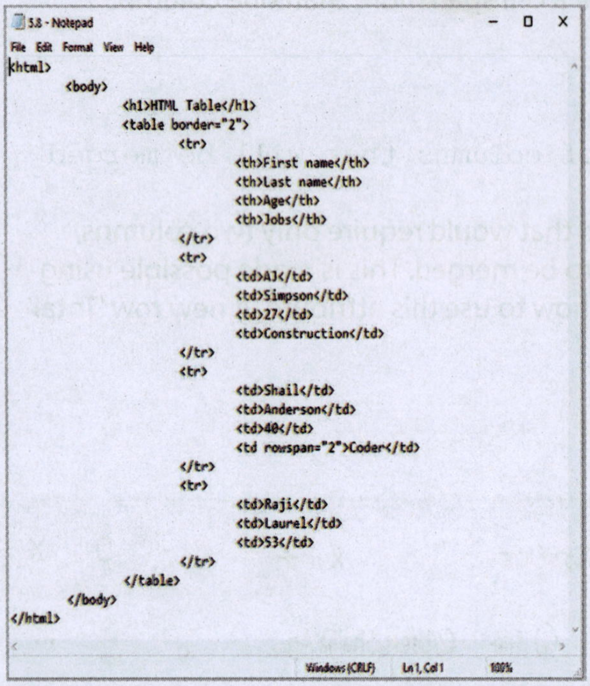

```
<html>
	<body>
		<h1>HTML Table</h1>
		<table border="2">
			<tr>
				<th>First name</th>
				<th>Last name</th>
				<th>Age</th>
				<th>Jobs</th>
			</tr>
			<tr>
				<td>AJ</td>
				<td>Simpson</td>
				<td>27</td>
				<td>Construction</td>
			</tr>
			<tr>

				<td>Shail</td>
				<td>Anderson</td>
				<td>40</td>
				<td rowspan="2">Coder</td>
			</tr>
			<tr>
				<td>Raji</td>
				<td>Laurel</td>
				<td>53</td>
			</tr>
		</table>
	</body>
</html>
```

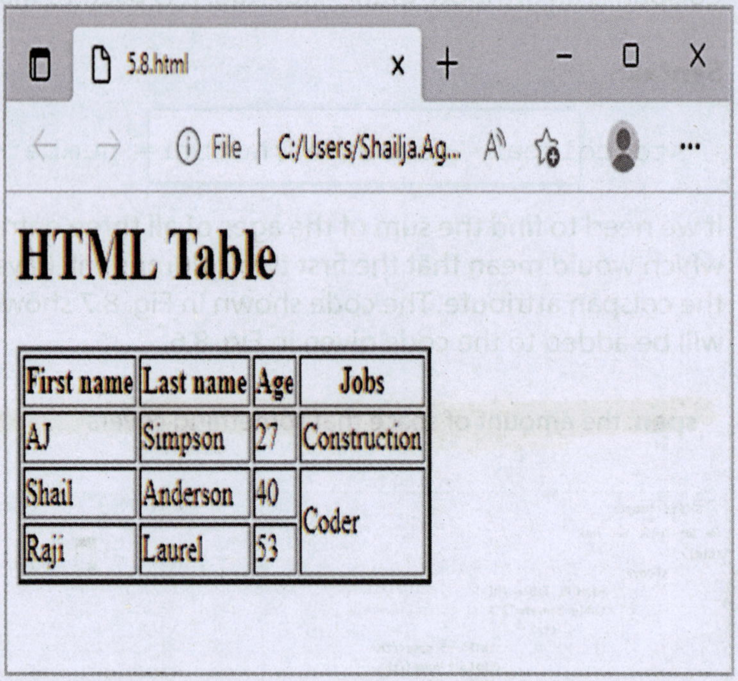

HTML Table

First name	Last name	Age	Jobs
AJ	Simpson	27	Construction
Shail	Anderson	40	Coder
Raji	Laurel	53	

Fig. 8.8 | *Table with the rowspan attribute*

Clear up!

Write an HTML code to create the table shown here:

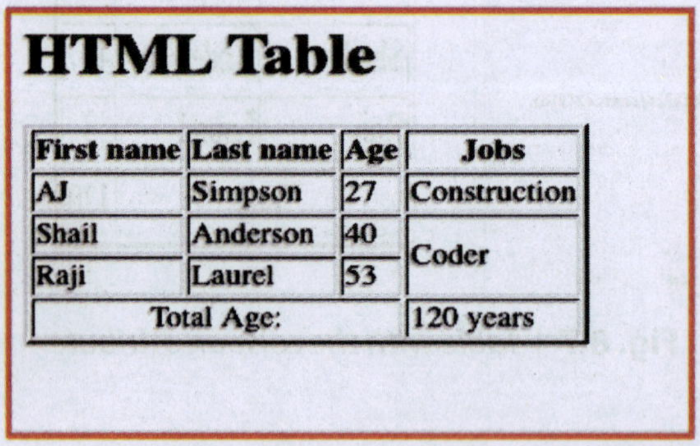

HTML Table

First name	Last name	Age	Jobs
AJ	Simpson	27	Construction
Shail	Anderson	40	Coder
Raji	Laurel	53	
Total Age:			120 years

Image Tag

A website consists of text, images, links and videos. Until now, we have just seen different ways of adding text to a website. Images add more value to a web page and make it look much more attractive.

Crank up! Technology Literacy

The path can be retrieved by right-clicking on the image and then selecting the Properties option.

The images in a web page can be inserted using the image tag <img>. Before using this tag, let us look at the various attributes of the image tag:

- **src** is the attribute for the img tag, which mentions the source of the picture.
- **Pic.jpg** is the name of the picture that will be picked up from the computer and displayed on the browser (Fig. 8.9). This element does not contain any content, and thus, the end tag is optional.
- The **path name** is the destination from where the picture will be picked up (in this case, where pic.jpg is located, i.e., the desktop).

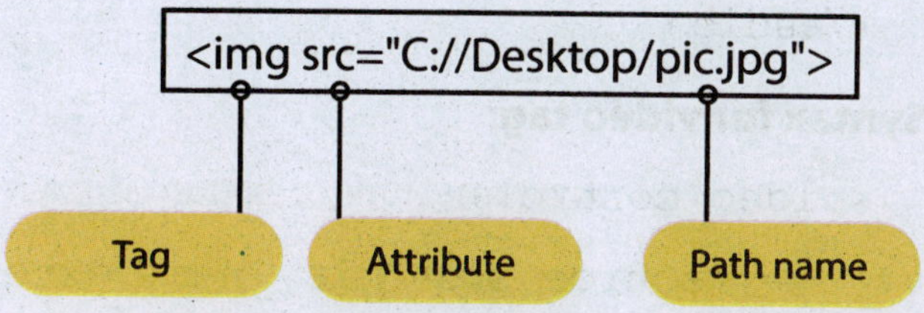

Fig. 8.9 | *Syntax of an <img> tag*

If the image is in the same location as the .html file, simply mention the file name in the source location as:

```
<img src="pic.jpg">
```

We can also use an image directly from the internet by specifying its web location:

```
<img src="https://i.ytimg.com/vi/MPV2METPeJU/dog.jpg">
```

Similar to src, the img tag has other attributes as well, such as width, height and alt (Fig. 8.10).

```
<img src="satya.jpg" height="100" width="200" alt= "Satya Nadella">
```

width and **height** are measured either in pixels or are given as percentage. One can adjust the size of the image accordingly. The **alt** attribute specifies an alternate text for the image, in case the image does not load.

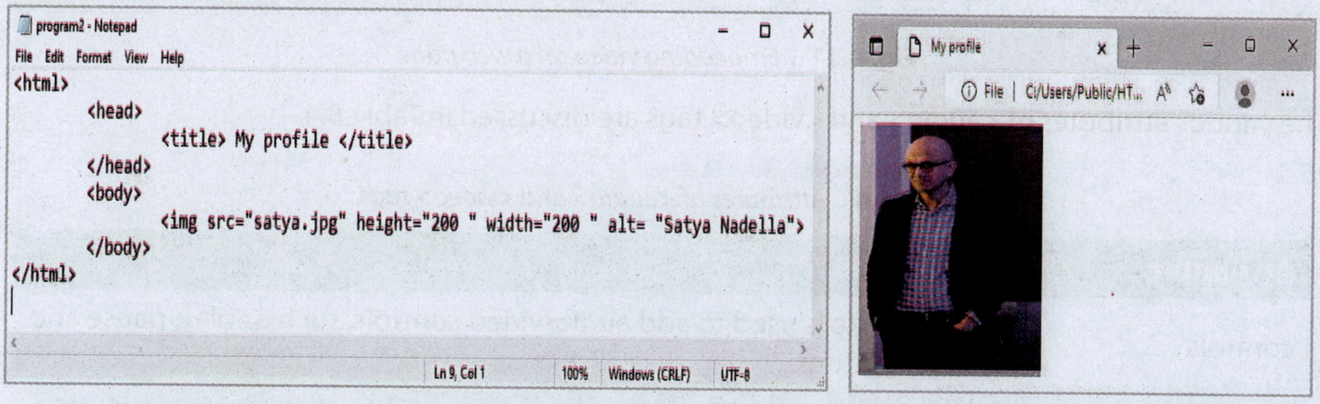

Fig. 8.10 | *Using the <img> tag*

Audio and Video Tags

HTML5 has made it very easy to add audio and video to a web page. No flash player is required to run this element. For this purpose, <audio> and <video> tags are used, respectively. These tags make it simple to add media to a website. Just like <img> tag, we need to set the src attribute to identify the media source and include a controls attribute, so that the user can play and pause the media. Any text written within the opening and closing tags is displayed only if the audio/video cannot be displayed on the browser.

Syntax for audio tag:

```
<audio controls>
        <source src="file _ name.extension">
</audio>
```

Syntax for video tag:

```
<video controls>
        <source src="file _ name.extension">
</video>
```

<source> tag is used to specify the destination of the audio/video file. It has to be used along with the src attribute, which specifies the path of the multimedia file. Some commonly used extensions of audio files are *.mp3*, *.ogg* and .wav, and those of video files are *.mp4*, *.webm* and *.ogg*.

For example, consider the HTML program and the corresponding output given in Fig. 8.11.

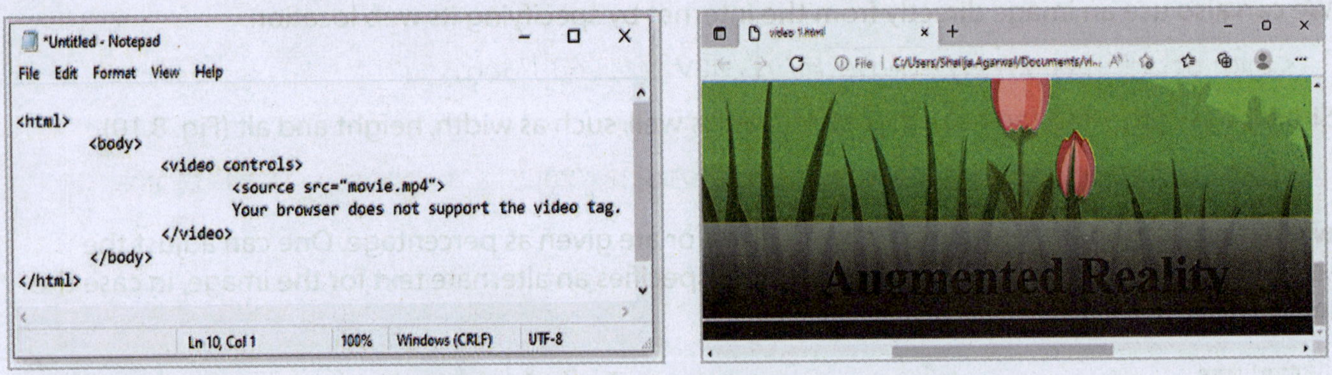

Fig. 8.11 | *Embedding video on a web page*

The various attributes of <audio> and <video> tags are discussed in Table 8.4.

Table 8.4 | *Attributes of <audio> and <video> tags*

Attributes	Description
controls	This attribute is used to add audio/video controls, such as play, pause and volume buttons.
autoplay	This attribute plays the multimedia automatically on the browser. It can be used instead of the controls attribute.
height and width	These are optional attributes that can be used to define the size of the video displayed.

Anchor Tag

Anchor tag is represented by <a> and is used to link one web page to another. It converts a text or an image into a hyperlink.

It is mostly used:

1. to move from one web page to another or to move on a different website.
2. to move from one web page to another within the same website.
3. to move from one section to another within the same web page.

The most important attribute for the <a> tag is **href** (hypertext reference), which specifies the entire destination path the link is pointing to (Fig. 8.12).

```
<a href ="https://www.google.com">Click here to go to Google</a>
```

When we click on the text inside the start and end anchor tags, we are directed to the specified link.

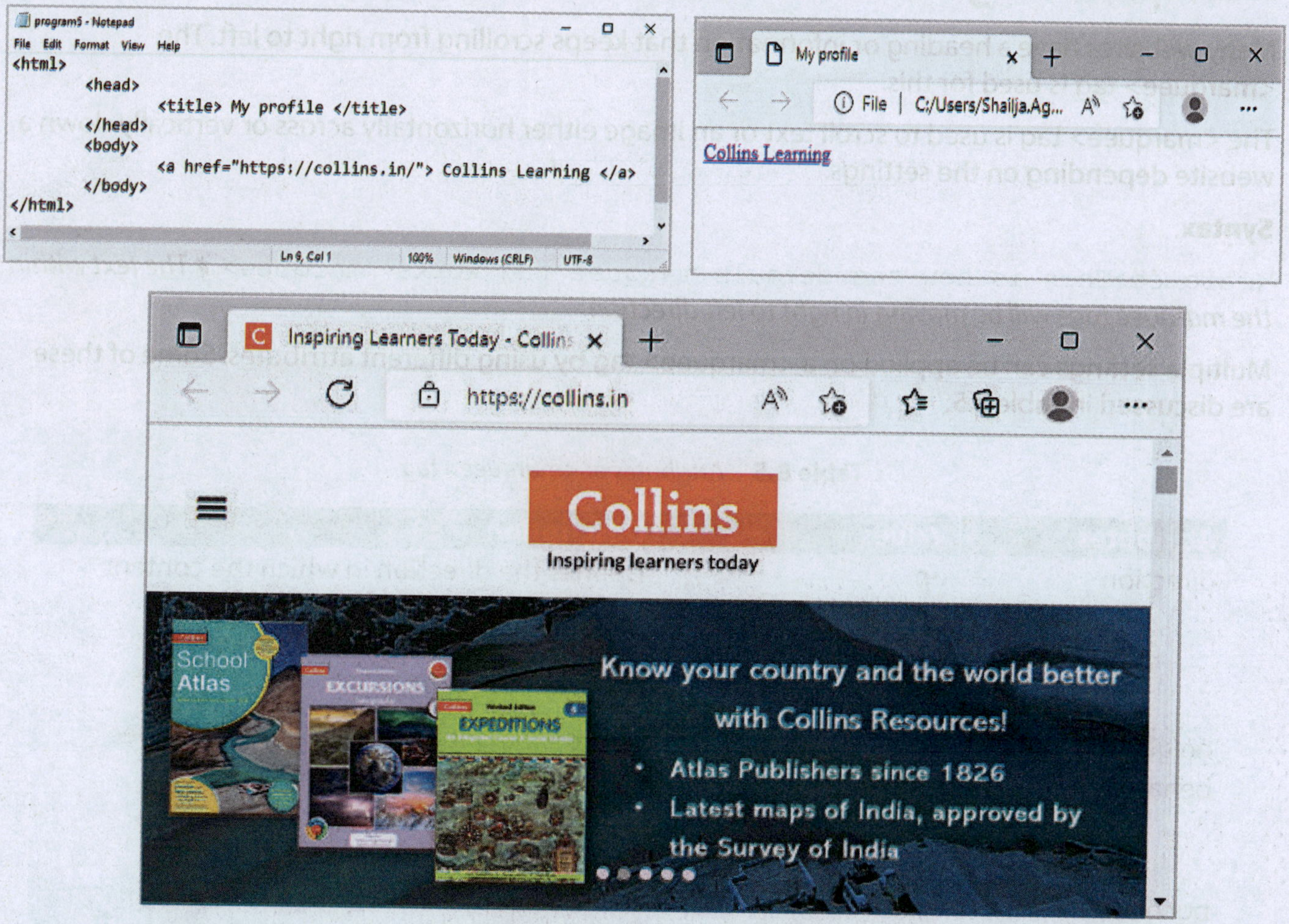

Fig. 8.12 | *Using the <a> tag*

Soak up!

An unvisited link is underlined and blue, while a visited link is underlined and purple.

Link up!

When you search something on Google or Bing, all the websites that are displayed in the searches are hyperlinks added using anchor tag.

Brush up!

Few tags such as <img> and <a> will not work without an attribute. Can you tell why?

____

____

Marquee Tag

Many websites have a heading or information that keeps scrolling from right to left. The <marquee> tag is used for this.

The <marquee> tag is used to scroll text or an image either horizontally across or vertically down a website depending on the settings.

Syntax:

`<marquee>This is how the default marquee tag works</marquee>` *# The text within the marquee tags will be moving in right to left direction*

Multiple settings can be applied on a <marquee> tag by using different attributes. Some of these are discussed in Table 8.5:

Table 8.5 | *Attributes of <marquee> tag*

Attributes	Values	Description
direction	up down right left	Defines the direction in which the content scrolls
height and width	pixels and %	Sets the height and width of the marquee
behavior	scroll slide alternate	Defines the type of scrolling
bgcolor	rgb(x,x,x) #xxxxxx color name	Gives a background colour to the scroll
hspace	pixels	Specifies horizontal space around the marquee
loop	number	Provides how many times the marquee will loop
vspace	pixels or percentage	Provides a vertical space
hspace	pixels or percentage	Provides a horizontal space
scrolldelay	seconds	Defines how long to delay between each jump
scrollamount	number	Determines the speed of the marquee

The syntax of adding the <marquee> tag with an attribute is given below:

```
<marquee direction="up"> This is how the marquee tag scrolls from down
to up </marquee> # The text within the marquee tags will be moving in
upward direction
```

Technology Literacy

Crank up!

The <Marquee> tag is usually used in websites for conveying important information or caution continuously on the website.

Today I learned!

- Lists are used to present data in a structured, clean manner. The <li> tag is used along to define lists in HTML.
- The <ol> tag defines an ordered list. Numbers, alphabets, roman numbers, etc., are used to represent this list. Numerical values are the default values taken by the <ol> tag.
- The <ul> tag defines an unordered list. Bullets, circles and squares are used to represent this list. Bullets are the default values taken by this tag.
- Attribute type is used to change the values of the list items.
- The <dl> tag represents the description list, which is used to define every list item in detail. It is used along with <dt> and <dd> tags.
- The <table> tag is used for adding tables to an HTML file.
- The <th>, <tr> and <td> tags are used to represent the table header, table row and table data, respectively.
- Colspan and rowspan attributes are used with the <td> tag to span the columns and rows of a table cell.
- The <img> tag is used for adding images to a webpage. This tag is used with the src attribute.
- The <audio> and <video> tags are used along with controls or autoplay attributes to add audio and/or video to a webpage. The destination of audio and video is determined by the <source> tag along with src attribute.
- The anchor <a> tag used to add hyperlinks to a webpage. This tag is used with the href attribute.
- The <marquee> tag is used to scroll text or an image either horizontally across or vertically down a website.

Revise and polish!

1. Tick (✓) the correct answer.

a. A(n) ______________ list is used when the sequence of the steps is important.

(i) ordered ☐ (ii) unordered ☐

(iii) description ☐ (iv) nested ☐

b. A description list is also called a (n)______________ list.

(i) attribute ☐ (ii) definition ☐ (iii) nested ☐ (iv) value ☐

c. Which of the following table attribute specifies the table row?

(i) <tr> ☐ (ii) <th> ☐ (iii) <td> ☐ (iv) th ☐

d. The <td> tag is used to make a cell span more than one ______________.

(i) table ☐ (ii) row ☐ (iii) column ☐ (iv) cell ☐

e. Which of the following is NOT an attribute of <audio> and <video> tags.

(i) controls ☐ (ii) autoplay ☐

(iii) autosubmit ☐ (iv) All of the above ☐

f. Which of the following tag is used to give destination of an audio file?

(i) source ☐ (ii) destination ☐ (iii) audio ☐ (iv) value ☐

g. Which of these attributes is used to get a bullet symbol in HTML?

(i) bullet ☐ (ii) circle ☐ (iii) round ☐ (iv) square ☐

h. The tag <th> is used to set the ______________.

(i) table header ☐ (ii) table body ☐ (iii) table html ☐ (iv) table cell ☐

i. Which of these is used to span a column in a table?

(i) colspan ☐ (ii) rowspan ☐ (iii) Both ☐ (iv) colorspan ☐

2. Fill in the blanks.

a. The ______________ tag creates a numbered list.

b. Description lists are represented using ______________ tags.

c. To change the direction of a scroll, ______________ is used.

d. The full form of <dd> is ______________.

e. Tables should be used with ______________ tags.

3. Match the following.

a.	ul	(i)	Merges rows
b.	ol	(ii)	Displays bullets
c.	rowspan	(iii)	Displays lists in the form of capital letters
d.	bullets	(iv)	Sets the behaviour of the <marquee> tag
e.	behavior	(v)	Default list item for unordered list

4. Write if the following is a tag or an attribute or a value.

a. a ________________ b. src ________________

c. li ________________ d. dt ________________

e. th ________________

5. Answer the following questions.

a. Which tag is used to add hyperlinks to a website? Give the syntax for the same.

b. What are the values one can use in ordered lists?

c. Give the difference between colspan and rowspan.

d. Explain a description list with example.

e. What is a marquee tag? Can you name any website where you have seen it?

6. Underline the errors in the following codes.

a.
```
<html>
 <body>
  <table>
   <th>
    <td>Fruits
    <td>Cost
   </th>
   <th>
    <td><Apples>
    <td>INR 150
   </th>
   <th>
    <td>Bananas
    <td>INR 20
   </th>
   </tr>
  </table>
</html>
```

b.
```
<html>
<h1>
<body>
MindChamp</h1>
   <img src= "logo.jpg"
   height= "100"
   width="200" alternate=
   "codingclass">
</body>
</html>
```

c.
```
<html>
<body>
<h2>My Shopping List</
  h2>
<p>I love to shop</p>
<ul>
  <li>Black cap
  <ul>
  <li>Red sneekers
  </li>
  <li> T-shirt</li>
  </ul>
</html>
```

Lab Activities

Experiential Learning

1. Write an HTML program that has an audio embedded within it.
2. Write an HTML program to display an informative page about your school. Add pictures of your school and videos from the sports day and annual day events.
3. Create a table in HTML with 3 columns and 5 rows. For each animal, display its name, picture, and whether it is a wild or a domestic animal.
4. Create a table in HTML with 2 columns and minimum 4 rows. Use table headers: Name of the bird and Image of the bird. Insert names and images of birds.
5. Create an HTML web page about your school. Try adding school pictures and videos from sports day/annual concerts.
6. Create a marquee on your HTML page.
   a. Ensure it says "Welcome to my first HTML Webpage" and scrolls from left to right and then from right to left.

Hint: Check the behaviour attribute

Can you control the speed and make the marquee move slower? How?

Think and Answer

Critical thinking

1. Sakshi tried to add a GIF to her HTML code using the <video> tag but was unable to do so. Can you tell why?

____

____

2. Sam has created a web page on which he has embedded a video clip. However, he is unable to see the play, pause and volume buttons. What can he add to make sure the buttons are visible along with the video?

____

____

3. Shreya used the <ul> tag to write a two-page algorithm for her class group project which she has shared with Swasti. Swasti is unable to follow the steps sequentially. What can you change to make sure Swasti finds it easier to follow the steps?

____

____

Chapter 9

Forms in HTML

After reading this chapter, I will be able to:

- ✔ Explain how to create a form in HTML.
- ✔ Describe how to use the <textarea>tag.
- ✔ Discuss the <input> and <select> tags.

Brainstorm and explore!

Here are two sample forms:

Login Form

Username
Password

Submit

Login Form

Username: [ ]
Password: [ ]
[Submit]

Which of these forms looks better and why? Write your answers in the space given below:

____

____

____

____

Most of us have email accounts. While setting up an email account or logging into one, we have to fill a sign up or sign in form. In this chapter, let us learn how those forms are created.

Forms in HTML

The <form> tag is used to create an HTML form for taking input from the user. The <form> tag, like other tags, is a part of the <body> tag.

Syntax:

```
<html>
    <body>
        <form>
            form elements
        </form>
    </body>
</html>
```

> **Link up!**
>
> Do you have your own email address?
>
> Do you remember filling up the sign up form used when you clicked on the **Sign up** button? Similarly, when you try to login into your account, you see a login form which asks you to enter your username and password.

An HTML form contains multiple form elements for text boxes, dropdown box, checkboxes and submit buttons. Let us learn about the tags used to create them.

<textarea> Tag

The <textarea> tag is used to create a multiple-line text box for input. It has an end tag </textarea> (Fig. 9.1).

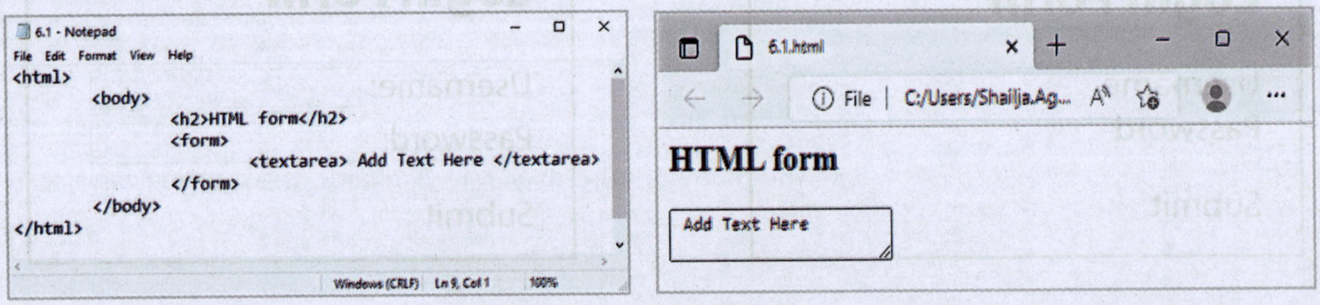

Fig. 9.1 | *The <textarea> tag*

To add fixed lines of rows and columns, the attributes **rows** and **cols** are used (Fig. 9.2)

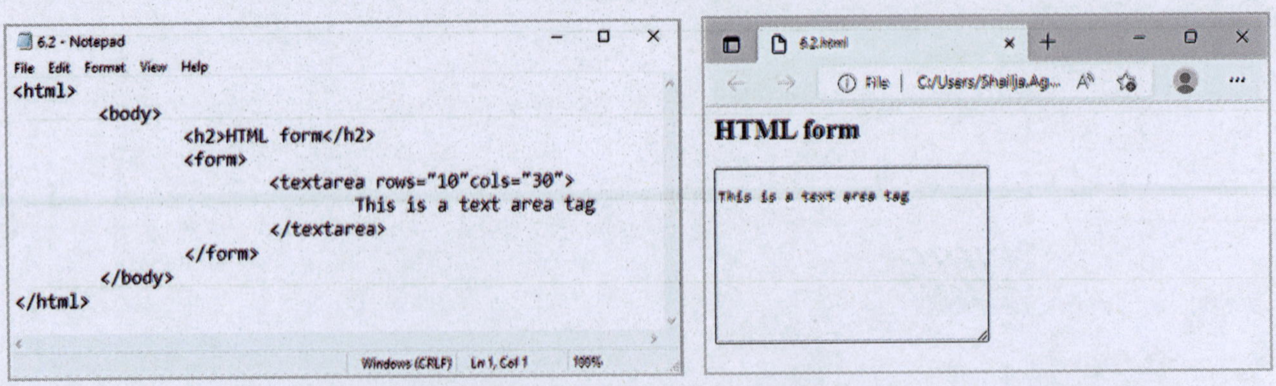

Fig. 9.2 | *Adding fixed lines of rows and columns.*

<input> Tag

The <input> element is the most commonly used element in a form. It is used along with a mandatory *type* attribute, which determines the output. Text, buttons, radio buttons, checkboxes and files can be added using the <input> tag. Let us learn how.

Single-line Text

`<input type="text">` creates a single-line text box for taking input from the user (Fig. 9.3).

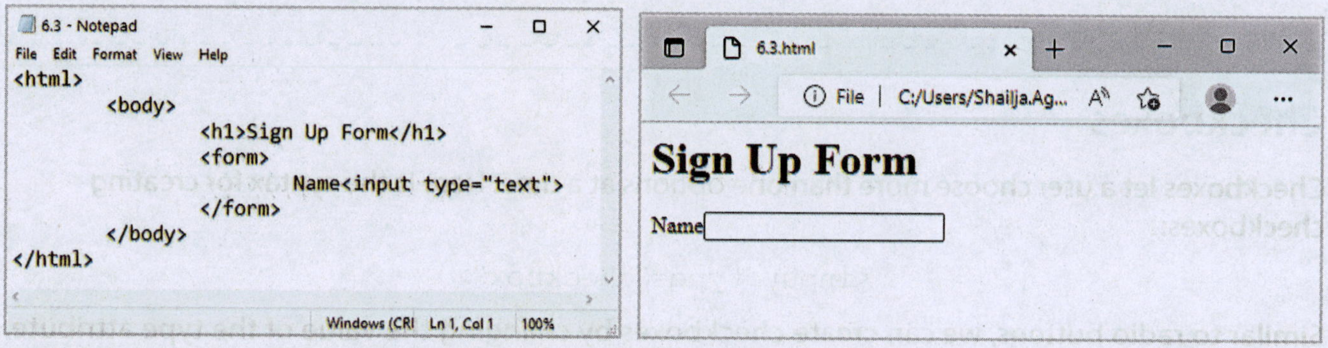

Fig. 9.3 | *Creating a single-line text box*

The *maxlength* attribute specifies the maximum number of characters allowed in an input field.

Syntax:

```
<input type="text" maxlength=25>
Enter your name</input>
```

Clear up!

The *value* attribute is optional and can add a default value in the text box.

What output will the following code give?

```
<input type="text" value="Soma">
```

Radio Buttons

Radio buttons let a user choose one of the many options available. Similar to the text, we can get radio buttons by changing the value of the type attribute.

`<input type="radio">` creates radio buttons (Fig. 9.4). The attribute **name** is mandatory for creating radio buttons.

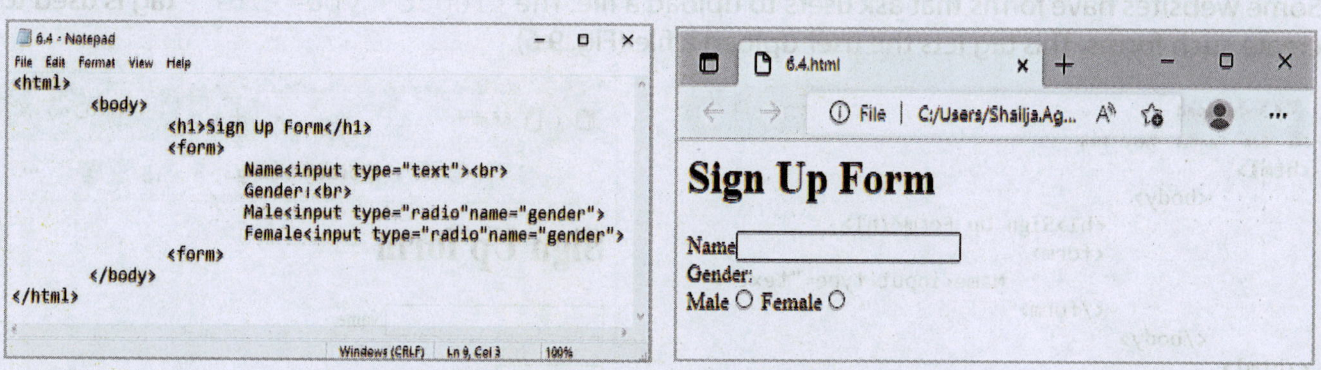

Fig. 9.4 | *Creating radio buttons*

A radio button cannot be used when there are more than one options to choose from.

That is when the checkbox comes in the picture.

Brush up!

For selecting hobbies in a form, would you use a radio button? Why or why not?

____

Checkboxes

Checkboxes let a user choose more than one options at a time. Here is the syntax for creating checkboxes:

```
<input type="checkbox">
```

Similar to radio buttons, we can create checkboxes by changing the value of the type attribute. But, unlike radio buttons, name is not a mandatory attribute for creating checkboxes (Fig. 9.5).

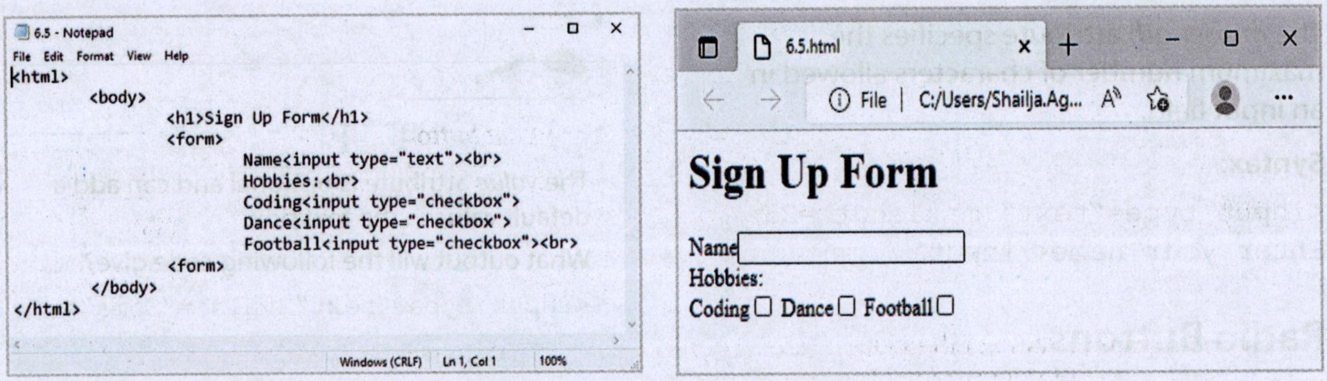

Fig. 9.5 | *Creating checkboxes*

Upload File

Some websites have forms that ask users to upload a file. The `<input type="file">` tag is used to create such forms. This tag lets the user upload a file (Fig. 9.6).

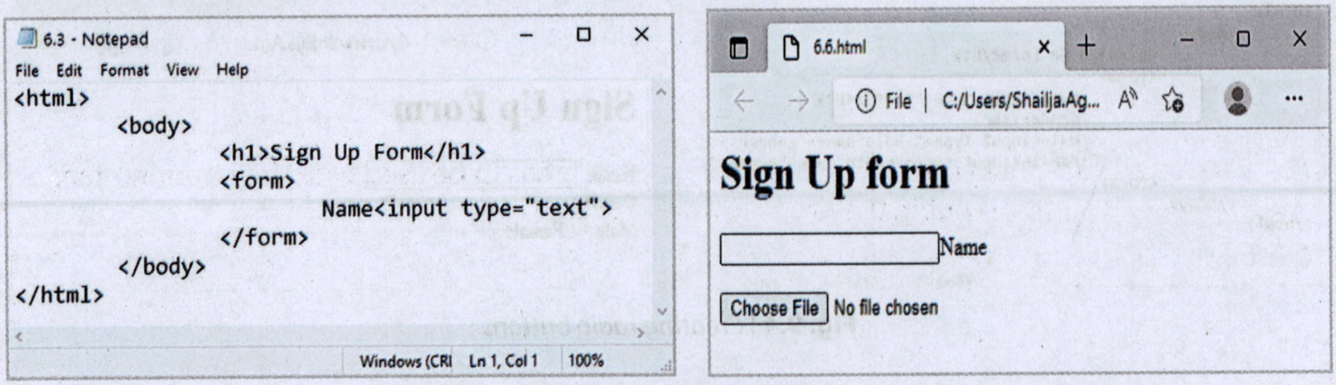

Fig. 9.6 | *Uploading a file*

Submit

Another use of the input tag is using the value *submit*.

```
<input type="submit">
```

The syntax given above creates a submit button as shown in Fig. 9.7.

Other than using the "submit" type, we can also change the type to "button", and add value "submit" to give the same results.

```
<input type="button" value="submit">
```

Soak up!

Multiple files can be added using the multiple attribute, as shown here:

```
<input type="file" multiple">
```

Use the Control key (Ctrl) to select more than one file.

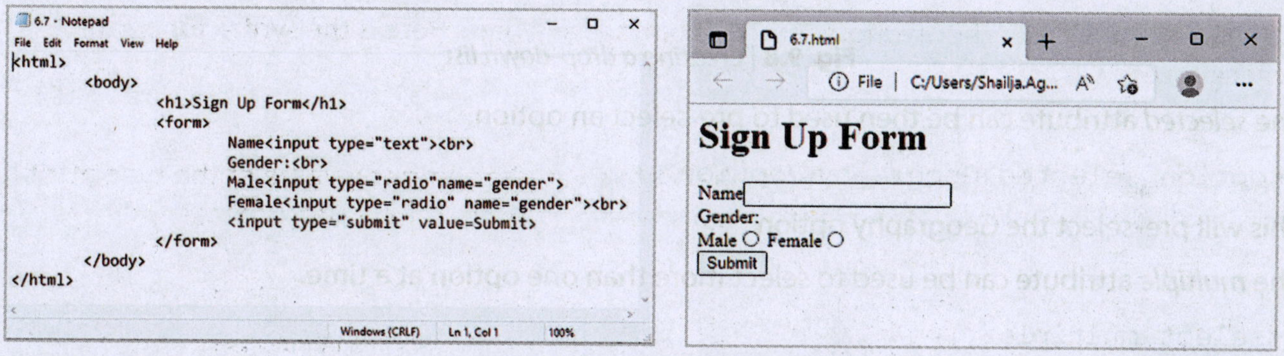

Fig. 9.7 | *Creating a Submit button*

Crank up!

By changing the value of the **value** attribute, we can create different types of buttons in the form.

```
<input type="button" value="Reset">.
```

Technology Literacy

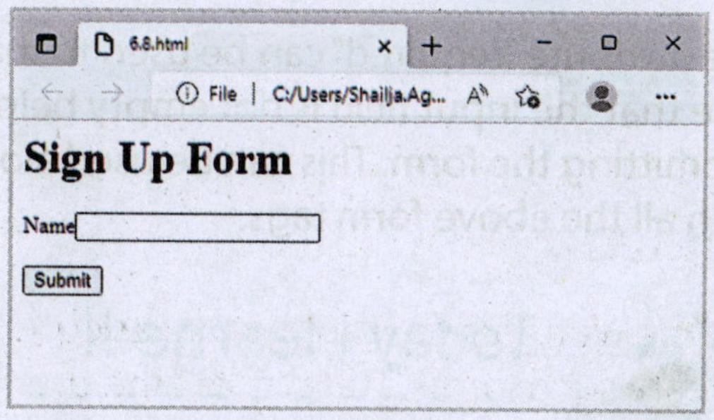

<Select> Tag

For creating a drop-down list, the <select> tag is used. It has to be used with the <option> tag, which defines options to put in the drop-down list.

Syntax:

```
<select>
    <option>Option that can be selected</option>
</select>
```

Both <select> and <option> tags have end tags. Figure 9.8 shows the output of the code using the <select> tag and its corresponding output.

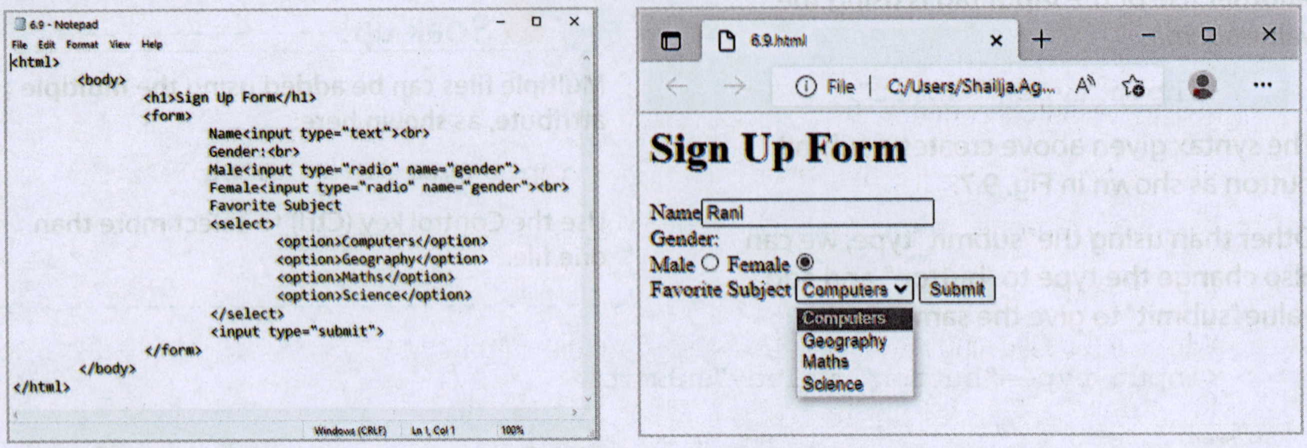

Fig. 9.8 | *Creating a drop-down list*

The *selected* attribute can be then used to pre-select an option.

```
<option selected>Geography</option>
```

This will pre-select the Geography option.

The *multiple* attribute can be used to select more than one option at a time.

```
<select multiple>
    <option>
        ...
    </option>
</select>
```

The attribute "required" can be used to make sure that the input field is not empty before submitting the form. This can be used along with all the above form tags.

Clear up!

What is the difference between a radio button and a checkbox? Give scenarios for the use of both of them.

Today I learned!

- In HTML, forms are created using the <form> tag.
- To get a multiline text input box, the <textarea> tag is used.
- The <input> tag is used to create a single-line text box, radio buttons, checkboxes and other buttons and lets us upload files in a form.
- The <textarea> tag is used to create a multiple-line text box for input.
- Radio buttons let a user choose one of the many options available.
- Checkboxes let a user choose more than one options at a time.
- The <select> tag is used to create a drop-down list.

Revise and polish!

Learning Skills

1. Tick (✓) the correct answer.

a. To choose multiple options, the ______________ is used.

(i) value ☐ (ii) select ☐ (iii) input ☐ (iv) textarea ☐

b. To create a form, the <form> tag is used within the ______________ tag.

(i) <input> ☐ (ii) <body> ☐ (iii) <head> ☐ (iv) <td> ☐

c. Which of the following attributes is used with the radio button?

(i) name ☐ (ii) type ☐ (iii) ID ☐ (iv) head ☐

d. Which of these tags is used to insert single-line text?

(i) <textarea> ☐ (ii) <input> ☐ (iii) <line> ☐ (iv) <colspan> ☐

e. The ______________ tag creates a drop-down list.

(i) <select> ☐ (ii) <option> ☐

(iii) <dropdown> ☐ (iv) <value> ☐

f. ______________ lets a user choose one of the many options available in the list.

(i) Radio ☐ (ii) Multibox ☐ (iii) Checkbox ☐ (iv) Multilist ☐

g. Which of these should be specified to add in input type?

(i) Upload ☐ (ii) File ☐ (iii) Text ☐ (iv) Value ☐

h. Which of these tags do not have an end tag?

(i) <form> ☐ (ii) <option> ☐ (iii) <input> ☐ (iv) <table> ☐

i. The __________ attribute can be used to select more than one option at a time in the <select> tag.

(i) multiple ☐ (ii) many ☐ (iii) option ☐ (iv) value ☐

2. Fill in the blanks.

a. The <input> tag is used in a form with the ____________ attribute.

b. The ____________ tag is used to insert multiline text.

c. The <select> tag has to be used along with the ____________ tag.

d. <input type="submit" value="reset"> will display ____________ text on the button.

e. The <select> tag is used to create a ____________ list.

f. The ____________ attribute specifies the maximum number of characters allowed in an input field.

3. **State whether the following statements are true (T) or false (F).**

a. The <form> tag is a part of the <body> tag. ☐

b. The attributes rows and cols are used to add fixed lines of images. ☐

c. The <input> element is used along with a mandatory type attribute. ☐

d. Radio buttons let a user choose one of the many options available. ☐

e. Both <select> and <option> tags have end tags. ☐

4. **In a sentence or two, describe what the following tags/attributes/values are used for.**

a. Selected

____

____

b. Name

____

____

c. Button

____

____

d. Checkbox

____

____

e. Textarea

____

____

5. **Answer the following questions.**

a. How is a drop-down list created in HTML?

b. What is the form tag used for? Write its syntax. Name any two form elements used with the form tag.

c. Which tags are used with the input tag to create checkboxes and radio buttons?

d. Write the differences between a radio button and a checkbox.

e. What is the <select> tag used for? Give an example

6. **Underline the errors in the following codes.**

a.
```
<html>
<body>
<h1></h1>
<form>
Age<input type="checkbox">
<b> Add a form text
</form>
</body>
</html>
```

b.
```
<body>
<h1>Checking radio button
<form>
Which of these is a streaming website
Youtube<input type="radio" >
Timesofindia<input type="radio" >
mercedes<input type="radio" >
<form>
</body>
</html>
```

c.
```
<html>
<body>
<h1>Sign Up Form
</h1>
<form>
Favorite company
<select>
<option>Amazon</option>
<option>Flipkart</option>
<option>MindChamp</option>
<option>Urban Ladder</option>
<input type="submit"></input>
</form>
</body>
</html>
```

Lab Activities

Experiential Learning

1. Sunetra wants to create a login form to enter the username and password of the user. Can you help her create it? Name the fields she will need in the login form.

____

____

2. Vivek has created the following form. He has forgotten the code for the same. Can you recreate it for him?

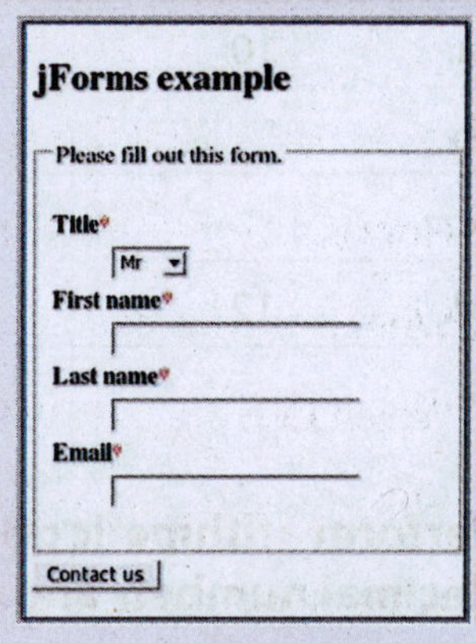

3. Sudhir has started a coding club and he wants to create a signup form that his classmates can fill out to join the club.

   Help him create the form by writing the code. Add at least four questions to the user.

Worksheet 1 (Chapters 1, 2 and 3)

Problem-solving

Critical Thinking

1. **Classify the following into internal/external hardware and input/output/storage devices, wherever applicable.**

	Name of device	Internal/External hardware	Input/Output/Storage device
a.	Motherboard 		
b.	Disk drive 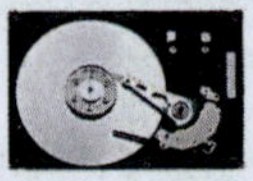		
c.	Speaker 		
d.	Headphones 		
e.	Laser printer 		

2. **Fill in the blanks to complete the number system table.**

S. No.	Decimal	Binary	Octal	Hexadecimal
a.	10		12	
b.		1111	17	
c.		1001		9
d.	12			C
e.			5	5

3. **Perform arithmetic operations on the following binary numbers. Convert them into decimal numbers and confirm if the answer is correct.**

a. 101 + 110

b. 110 + 001

c. 101 – 001

d. 111 – 101

4. Match the following cables with their respective ports.

a.	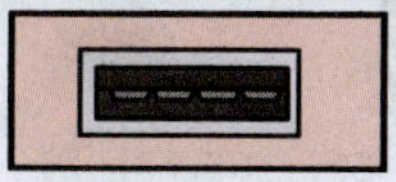	(i)	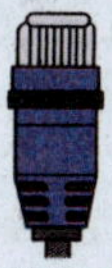
b.	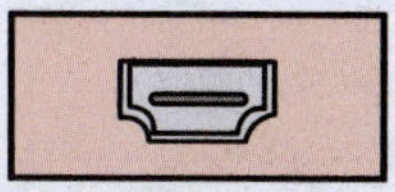	(ii)	
c.	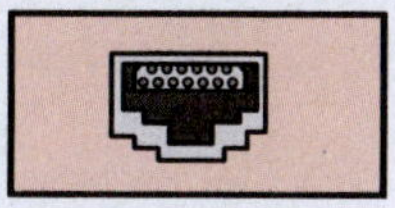	(iii)	
d.	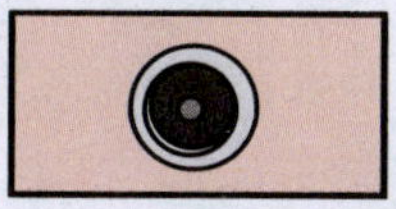	(iv)	

5. Identify the types of malware(s) in the following scenarios.

a. Gauri downloaded a video received as an email attachment from an unknown person. As the days went by, more and more files on her system started getting corrupted or deleted.

____

b. Raman, an IT official, received an email from an unknown person saying that he has gained access to Raman's customer database. The person is threatening Raman to pay him ₹50 lakh otherwise he will make the data public.

____

c. Lata downloaded a free antivirus software online and installed it on her computer. Whenever she scans the computer, the software detects unusual virus in system and asks for money to delete these.

____

d. Ira downloaded a software online. Along with this, a bundle of other software got downloaded, one of which might be infected.

____

6. Tick the point(s) you usually follow in the antivirus software installed on your computer.

a. Run a quick scan of the system every now and then. ☐

b. Delete the potential threats detected by the antivirus. ☐

c. Keep the firewall on. ☐

d. Scan the entire system every week. ☐

e. Keep the antivirus updated. ☐

Worksheet 2 (Chapters 4, 5 and 6)

Critical Thinking

India Focus (IF)

1. Classify the following passwords as weak or strong.

a.	abc123	
b.	Qwerty9870	
c.	Summer29*	
d.	I-love-Rabbits&Cats	
e.	%fg34	
f.	bg12ok&**	
g.	football%	

2. Highlight the dos for a netizen and correct the ones which are wrong.

a. Forwarding a WhatsApp message about a recent news on change in RBI guidelines sent to you by your cousin.

____

____

b. Ankur recently created a new social media account to make friends. He adds anyone who sends him a friend request.

____

____

c. Ankita shared her Gmail password with her brother so she does not forget it in future.

____

____

d. Reeth and Mehar know each other through a gaming website. Mehar sends Reeth a link with the subject "Tricks to reach level 55 no one wants you to know!!!" on the chat. Reeth is stuck on level 50 for one whole week. She should click the link and see what happens.

____

____

e. Ila's school friend has recently posted a link that explains a scheme to earn $25000 on Instagram. Ila immediately calls her friend on the phone to confirm if her friend has clicked on the link.

____

____

3. Look on the internet and create a list of all the endangered and extinct species as of 2022 in MS Excel. Add the following columns: Name of Animal, Region they belong to, Status (Endangered, Threatened, Delisted, Extinct), Reason. Add at least 20 rows and 4 columns.

Ensure the font colour of the extinct species is red and the highly endangered species is orange. Save the file as endangered.xlxs.

4. Create an Excel sheet to make your guest list and the food items required for your birthday party. Once completed, answer the following questions.

a. Write the column name where you have mentioned the names of the guests. ________________

b. Mention the rows in which the food items are mentioned. ________________

c. Write the cell address having the name of your best friend. ________________

5. Help your mother to create a daily expense tracker using MS Excel. As a 15-day project, track all the daily expenses at home along with your parents. Categorize every spend into food, clothing, loans, etc. Use formulas to calculate the total spend in each category.

6. India is vast and has different climatic zones in different parts of the country. As per a study carried out, India can be divided into six climatic zones, namely, hot and dry, warm and humid, moderate, cold and cloudy, cold and sunny, and composite.

Working in groups of six, create an Excel sheet to categorize each state and union territory of India into the respective climatic zone. Research thoroughly before entering data into the sheet as many states could be a mix of different climates.

Create a presentation of the information collated by the group and present it to the class.

Worksheet 3 (Chapters 7, 8 and 9)

Technology Literacy

Critical Thinking

1. Read the following table and answer the questions given below.

Name	Roll No.	Birth Date	Permanent Address	New Admission
Sumant	5	10/10/1994	B-5, Venkatesh Chambers, Prescot Road, Fort, Mumbai	Yes
Prashant	15	3/4/1994	9, A, Bhide Comp, Datta Mandir Rd, Bhandup(w), Mumbai	No
Hemant	25	6/6/1993	C403 , Odyssey, Raheja Vihar, Chandivali, Powai, Mumbai	No
Manasi	7	10/8/1993	A wing, 2003, Sunrise, Hiranandani Gardens, Powai, Mumbai	No

a. Which field could be identified as a primary key? ____________________

b. What are the data types used for each field?

Name	Roll No.	Birth Date	Permanent Address	New Admission

c. We need to add a new column "Gender" to the right of New Admission. Give the steps to do so.

d. What will be the data type for the new column?

2. A school database is created with the name "Happy Valley School". Multiple grade-wise records or tables have been created at the time of admissions. The class teacher of Grade 7, Mrs. Roy, wants to access students' records to find the total number of students in her class. Can you give the steps to help her out? Which of the two ways for query creation would you prefer and why?

3. Create a database for your classroom. Create separate records for the different clubs you have, such as coding club, nature club, etc. Accordingly, add students to those tables. Ensure all the students in your class have been added to the database.

Fields to be added are given here:

Name	Roll No.	Gender

Once completed, compare with your classmate's database and see if you have entered all the necessary tables.

4. **Create a table in HTML to list the different planets in the solar system. Try to add the following information to the table:**

Name of the planet	Description	Image	Video/Audio link

Can you create something similar in MS Excel as well? If yes, create a worksheet with similar information. List the differences between the worksheet and webpage created.

5. **Sumita wants to create multiple databases. Can you help Sumita with the fields she can add in each database? Underline the primary key for each database.**

	Database	Fields
a.	Clothing store	
b.	Tourism website	
c.	India's heritage sites	
d.	Vegetable vendors	

6. **Underline the mistakes in the following HTML program and rewrite the write code on the right hand side.**

```
<html>
<body>
RSVP FOR ASTHA'S BIRTHDAY PARTY</h2>
 Name:
 <input type="text" maxlegnth =
 1><br><br>
 What kind of food do you prefer? <br>
 Veg<input type="radio" >
 NonVeg<input type="radio">
 <br><br>
 Will you be joining the party on 21st
 March? <br>
 <select>
 <option>Yes
 <option>No
 </select>
 <br><br>
 <input type=submit value="Submit">
</form>
<p>If you are joining us for the
celebration, kindly be there at the
venue at 6:00 pm sharp for a surprise
show </p>
</body>
</html>
```

7. Aditya added the three fields in a form as shown here:

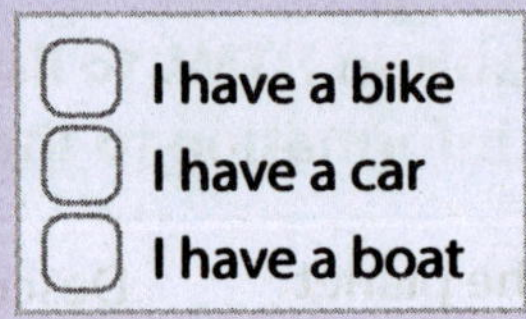

a. Name the tags used to create this form.

b. Ankur created the fields shown here:

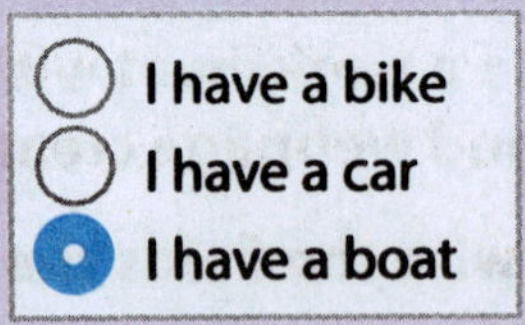

What is the difference between the two?

c. What tag should be used to add a heading to a form?

d. Is a separate HTML tag required to insert a Submit button in the end of the form? If yes, name it?

Additional Worksheet

Problem-solving | Critical Thinking

1. **Fill in the correct operators to make these statements true. There may be more than one way of doing this.**

   a. 5 ____ 10 = 50
   b. 2 ___ 4 ___ 6 = 0
   c. 10 ___ 10 ___ 10 = 10
   d. 100 ___ 10 ___ 500 ___ 500 ____ 1000 = 2000
   e. 111 ___ 222 ___ 333 ___ 444 = 1110
   f. 50 __ 2 __ 100 ___ 100 = 200

2. **Sam and his friends are playing a game in which they have to find something common between two or more words from the following grid. Then they have to come up with a new word that links the group of words.**

horse	bed	lamp	fire	green
bag	bench	water	vehicle	shirt
speak	hall	bread	table	dates
music	lights	celebrate	gold	stone
ticket	elephants	flower	stage	road

Sam and his friends have already played two rounds, as given in the following table. Continue playing the game and fill the table.

Two word links	Three word links	Four word links
1. music and hall - concert	1. fire, water, and vehicle - firefighters	1. table, dates, bread, and water - snack
2.	2.	2.
3.	3.	3.

3. **Lead the rabbit to the carrot.**

   Now write an algorithm describing the path.

   You can use these words: go straight, take left, take right, go down, go up

Fun Activity

We have learnt about ASCII codes in Chapter 2 of this book. Here is the complete sheet of ASCII codes and their binary equivalents for all the letters.

Letter	ASCII Code	Binary	Letter	ASCII Code	Binary
a	97	1100001	A	65	1000001
b	98	1100010	B	66	1000010
c	99	1100011	C	67	1000011
d	100	1100100	D	68	1000100
e	101	1100101	E	69	1000101
f	102	1100110	F	70	1000110
g	103	1100111	G	71	1000111
h	104	1101000	H	72	1001000
i	105	1101001	I	73	1001001
j	106	1101010	J	74	1001010
k	107	1101011	K	75	1001011
l	108	1101100	L	76	1001100
m	109	1101101	M	77	1001101
n	110	1101110	N	78	1001110
o	111	1101111	O	79	1001111
p	112	1110000	P	80	1010000
q	113	1110001	Q	81	1010001
r	114	1110010	R	82	1010010
s	115	1110011	S	83	1010011
t	116	1110100	T	84	1010100
u	117	1110101	U	85	1010101
v	118	1110110	V	86	1010110
w	119	1110111	W	87	1010111
x	120	1111000	X	88	1011000
y	121	1111001	Y	89	1011001
z	122	1111010	Z	90	1011010

Write your name in binary using the above sheet.

______________________ ______________________

Now, let us make a binary bracelet for your name.

Materials required: Beads in three different colours, ribbon

Method: Follow the method given here to make the binary bracelet:

1. Pick beads to represent 1, 0 and the space between the letters. For example, pink beads will represent 1, yellow beads will represent 0 and blue beads will represent the space between letters.
2. Arrange all the beads as per the letters in your name. Insert two blue beads to separate your first and last names.
3. Thread the ribbon through the beads.

Yeah! Your binary bracelet is complete .

CLASS 7

QUESTION PAPER SET A

NCO

SOF NATIONAL CYBER OLYMPIAD 2021-22

DO NOT OPEN THIS BOOKLET UNTIL ASKED TO DO SO

Total Questions: 50 | Time: 1 hr.

Guidelines for the Candidate

1. You will get additional ten minutes to fill up information about yourself on the OMR Sheet, before the start of the exam.
2. Write your **Name, School Code, Class, Roll No.** and **Mobile Number** clearly on the **OMR Sheet** and do not forget to sign it. We will share your marks / result and other information related to SOF exams on your mobile number.
3. The Question Paper comprises three sections:

   Logical Reasoning (10 Questions), **Computers and Information Technology** (35 Questions) and **Achievers Section** (5 Questions).

   Each question in Achievers Section carries 3 marks, whereas all other questions carry one mark each.
4. All questions are compulsory. There is no negative marking. Use of calculator is not permitted.
5. There is only ONE correct answer. Choose only ONE option for an answer.
6. To mark your choice of answers by darkening the circles on the OMR Sheet, use **HB Pencil** or **Blue / Black ball point pen** only. E.g.

   Q.16: Which of the following is a type of printer?

   A. Cathode Ray Tube B. Light Emitting Diode

   C. Thermal Flatbed D. Liquid Crystal Display

   As the correct answer is option C, you must darken the circle corresponding to option C on the OMR Sheet. 16. Ⓐ Ⓑ ● Ⓓ
7. Rough work should be done in the blank space provided in this booklet.
8. Return the OMR Sheet to the invigilator at the end of the exam.
9. Please fill in your personal details in the space provided on this page before attempting the paper.

SOF

SCIENCE OLYMPIAD FOUNDATION

Inspiring Young Minds Through Knowledge Olympiads

Name:..

SOF Olympiad Roll No.:.. Contact No.:..

1. Which of the following Venn diagrams best represents the relationship amongst, 'Triangles, Quadrilaterals and Rectangles'?

A. 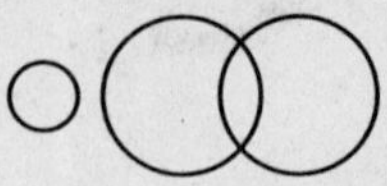

B. 

C. 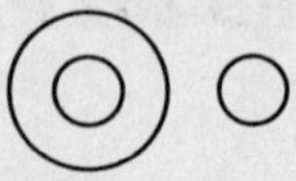

D. 

2. Count the number of triangles formed in the given figure.

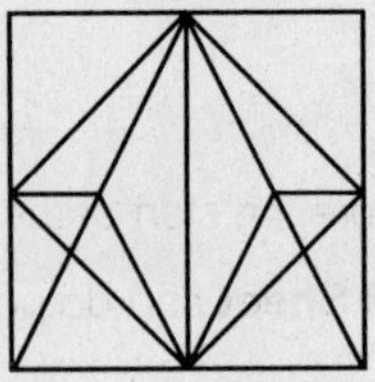

A. 28
B. 30
C. 27
D. More than 30

3. Which of the following options will complete the given letter series?

MOT, SRV, XVX, _?_, EGB

A. BZZ
B. BAZ
C. BAX
D. ABZ

4. In a class of 45 students, Harshit is at 7th position from the top and Nitin is at 9th position from the bottom. If Priyanka is placed exactly between them, then find the position of Priyanka from the top.

A. 21st
B. 22nd
C. 23rd
D. 32nd

5. Pointing towards a man, Krishna said, "He is the father-in-law of the wife of my father". How is the man related to Krishna?

A. Grandson
B. Father
C. Brother
D. Grandfather

6. Given question consists of a set of three figures X, Y and Z showing a sequence of folding of a piece of paper. Fig. (Z) shows the manner in which the folded paper has been cut. Select a figure from the options which would most closely resembles the unfolded form of Fig. (Z).

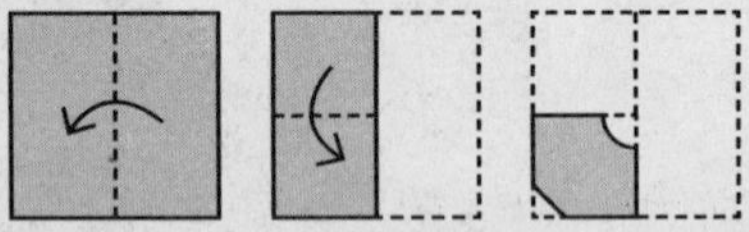

X Y Z

A. 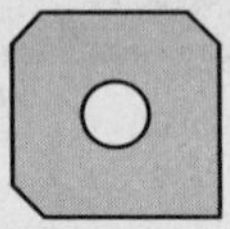

B. 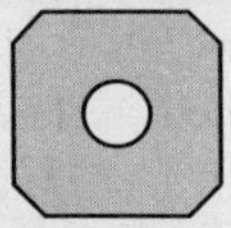

C. 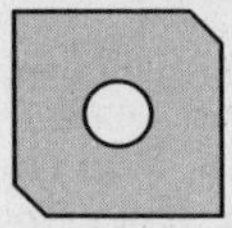

D. 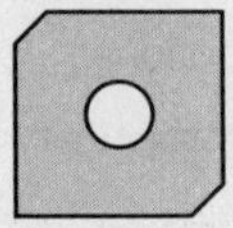

7. Which of the following figures satisfies the same conditions of placement of the dots as in the given figure?

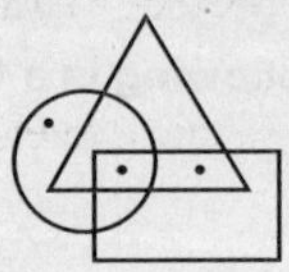

A. 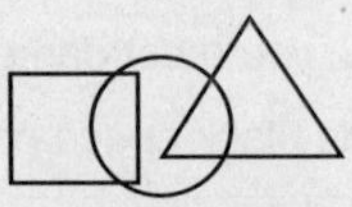

B. 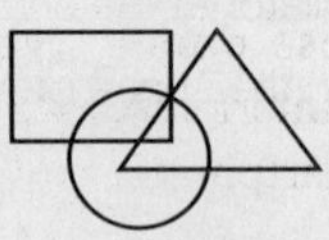

C. 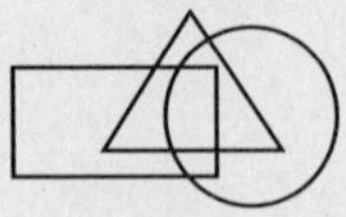

D. 

8. Vandana walks 25 m towards North. Then she turns towards her left and walks 20 m. She then turns to her right and walks 25 m. She again turns towards

her left and walks 15 m. Which direction is Vandana facing now?

A. East
B. West
C. North
D. South

9. Select the correct mirror image of the given combination of letters and numbers.

Mirror

A. 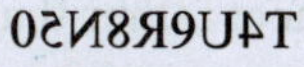
B. 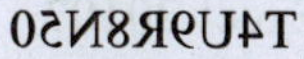
C. 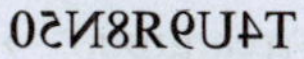
D. 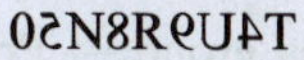

10. Select a figure from the options which will continue the same series as established by the Problem Figures.

Problem Figures

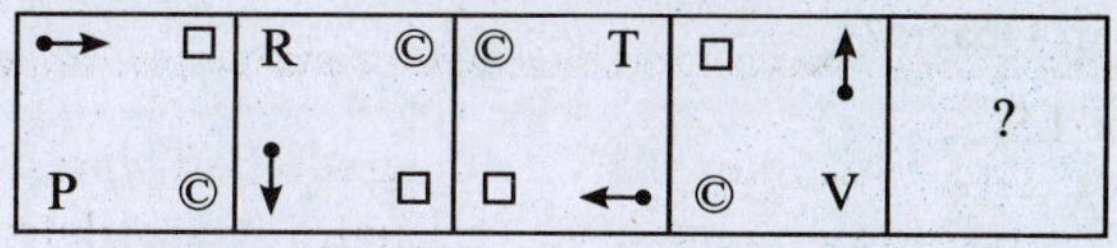

A. 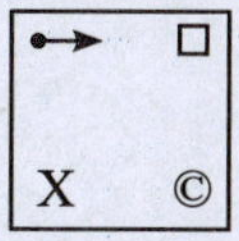

B. 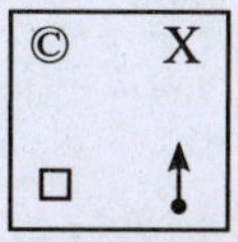

C. 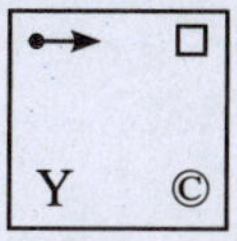

D. 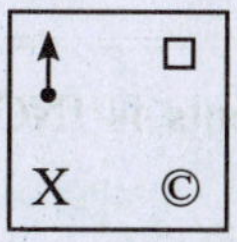

COMPUTERS AND INFORMATION TECHNOLOGY

11. Identify the following device.

- It is a hands-free speaker.
- It can also connect with Wi-Fi network and Bluetooth.
- It is virtual assistant developed by Amazon.

A. Alexa
B. Siri
C. Sophia
D. Google Assistant

12. ________ are wireless access points, typically in public locations, that provide internet access to mobile devices such as laptop or smartphone.

A. MAN
B. Hotspots
C. Datapack
D. LAN

13. Which of the following statements is CORRECT about Loaders?

A. It is a major component of an operating system that ensures all necessary programs and libraries are loaded.
B. It places the cache memory and programs into the main memory.
C. It is used to combine two separate programs.
D. It allocates memory location and brings programs into memory.

14. Identify the following.

- It is an expansion component used in computers to receive and send audio.
- It can be configured and utilized with the help of a software application and a device driver.
- It converts incoming digital audio data into analog audio.

A. Speaker
B. Sound card
C. Headphone
D. Woofer

15. Match the networking terms given in Column-I with their descriptions given in Column-II.

Column-I	Column-II
(a) Host computer	(i) Network protocol
(b) Peer	(ii) A computer circuit board
(c) NIC	(iii) A powerful, centralized computer system
(d) TCP/IP	(iv) A self-sufficient computer

A. (a) – (i), (b) – (iii), (c) – (ii), (d) – (iv)
B. (a) – (ii), (b) – (iii), (c) – (i), (d) – (iv)
C. (a) – (iii), (b) – (iv), (c) – (i), (d) – (ii)
D. (a) – (iii), (b) – (iv), (c) – (ii), (d) – (i)

16. What would be the output of the following program in Qbasic?

```
CLS
A = -5
B = 1
DO WHILE B < = 10
PRINT A;
A = A + 1
B = B + 1
LOOP
END
```

A. –5 –4 –3 –2 –1
B. –5 –4 –3 –2 –1 0 1 2 3 4
C. 0 1 2 3 4 5 6 7 8 9
D. –5 –4 –3 –2 –1 5 4 3 2 1

17. Which of the following statements is INCORRECT regarding Registers?

A. They are used to quickly accept, store and transfer data and instructions that are being used immediately by CPU.
B. It is a special, high-speed storage area or a temporary storage area built into a CPU.
C. They refer to the group of latches that store a single character.
D. They may hold temporary deleted data from recycle bin.

18. ________ is a search engine that sends queries to several search engines and either aggregates the results into one master list or categorizes the results by the search engines they come from.

A. Web search engine
B. Metasearch engine
C. Networking engine
D. Beta search engine

19. In which of the following type of network topologies, various star networks are interconnected via bus networks as shown in the given image?

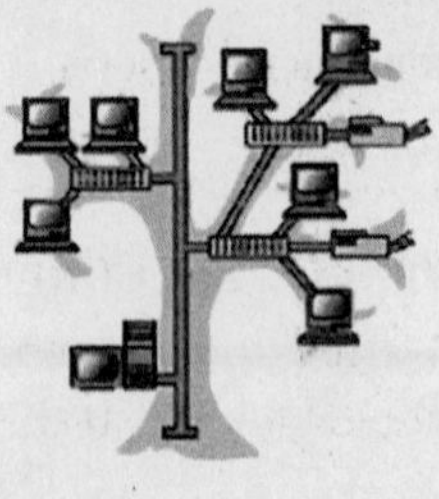

A. Hub topology
B. Ring topology
C. Mesh topology
D. Tree topology

20. Identify the following printer.

- It is a type of non-impact printer.
- It prints one page at a time, hence it is also referred as page printer.
- It uses toner to print on paper.

A. Band printer
B. Laser printer
C. Chain printer
D. Dot-matrix printer

21. Which of the following options can be used to print a specific selection on a worksheet rather than printing the entire worksheet in MS-Excel 2010?

A. Margin tab → Set Print Area group → Print
B. Size tab → Set Print Area group → Print
C. Print Area tab → Set Print Area group → Print
D. Page Layout tab → Page Setup group → Print Area → Set Print Area

22. Which of the following methods protect can be used to sensitive data by converting it into the secret code that hides true meaning of information?

A. Encryption
B. Copyright
C. Firewall
D. Captcha

23. What would be the output of the following program in Qbasic?

```
SCREEN 7
COLOR 4, 14
CLS
LINE (160, 30) – (250, 180), 4
LINE (250, 180) – (70, 180), 2
LINE (70, 180) – (160, 30), 1
END
```

A. Square
B. Isosceles triangle
C. Triangle
D. Right Angle

24. Which of the following statements is CORRECT regarding fifth generation of computer?

A. The main goal of this generation is to develop the devices which could respond to natural language input and are capable of self learning and self organization.

B. The UNIVAC and ENIAC computers are examples of this generation of computer.

C. The development of the integrated circuit was completed in this generation of computer.

D. They were often enormous in size and take up the entire room.

---

25. What would be the output of the given formula in MS-Excel 2010?

=MOD(5,2)

A. 0

B. 1

C. TRUE

D. FALSE

---

26. Identify the network cable from the given image.

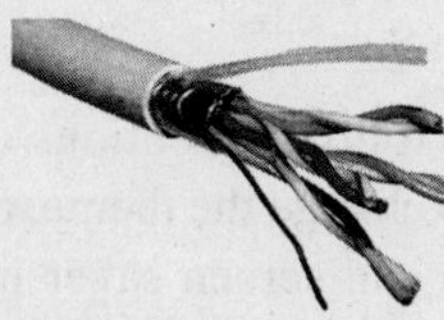

A. Coaxial cable

B. Fiber optic cable

C. Twisted pair cable

D. Radio transmission cable

---

27. The given icon is used to _________ in a document of MS-Word 2010.

A. Record Macro

B. View Macro

C. Switch Macro

D. Pause Macro

---

28. Which of the following hardware is used to read the information from the stripe of magnetic material present on credit cards?

A. QR reader

B. Magnetic stripe reader

C. Barcode reader

D. Digital reader

---

29. Cell phone network and satellite communication network are examples of ____________.

A. Wireless network

B. Wired network

C. Massive network

D. Light wave network

---

30. What would be the output, if you type the given formula in cell C1 in MS-Excel 2010?

=$A$1+$B$1

	A	B	C
1	10	5	?
2	20	15	?
3	15	25	?
4			

A. 15 15 15

B. 15 25 20

C. 15 35 40

D. #value #value #value

---

31. Which of the following is an area in the main memory that is used to temporarily store or hold the data that is being transmitted either between two devices or between a device and an application?

A. Defragmentation

B. Buffer

C. Operating system

D. Booting

---

32. Identify the following.

- A computer virus that infects a storage device's master boot record (MBR).
- It exists on storage media such as hard drives or occasionally CDs and DVDs.

A. Boot sector virus

B. File injector virus

C. Polymorphic virus

D. Web scripting virus

---

33. Select the INCORRECT match.

A. Supercomputer - IBM summit

B. Optical storage - Floppy disk

C. Notebook - MacBook

D. Search Engine - Bing

---

34. Seema wants to type the names of successive months or days in a row or a column. Which of the following options would she use in MS-Excel 2010?

A. Formatting numbers

B. Formatting cell

C. Auto Fill

D. Filter

35. Which of the following options states the INCORRECT difference between function and formula in MS-Excel 2010?

	Function	Formula
A.	It is a predefined calculation.	It is an equation designed by a user.
B.	It is a piece of code designed to calculate specific values and are used inside formula.	It contains values, references to cells, defined names and functions.
C.	It begins with "=" sign.	It always begins with capital letters only.
D.	Examples of functions are =Sum( ), =Min( ), =Max( ).	Example of formulas are =A3+C9, =45+25, = A9+B7–(5×2)+5.

36. What would be the output of the following program in Qbasic?

```
CLS
For i = 5 to 1 STEP -1
For j = 1 To i
PRINT j;
NEXT j
PRINT
NEXT i
END
```

A.
```
1 2 3 4 5
1 2 3 4
1 2 3
1 2
1
```

B.
```
1
1 2
1 2 3
1 2 3 4
1 2 3 4 5
```

C.
```
5 4 3 2 1
5 4 3 2
5 4 3
5 4
5
```

D.
```
5
5 4
5 4 3
5 4 3 2
5 4 3 2 1
```

37. When evaluating magnetic tapes, which of the following statements does NOT hold true?

A. Data on a tape is accessed and processed sequentially.

B. It is a secondary storage device.

C. It is the fastest medium for storing and accessing data.

D. The surface can record data by magnetization.

38. Identify the following feature of MS-Word 2010.

- It can point to other web pages, web sites, graphics files, sounds, e-mail addresses, and other locations.
- It is usually underlined and appeared as a different color.

A. Macros

B. Hyperlink

C. Bookmark

D. Mail Merge

39. Which of the following category view of control panel in Windows 7 will help to adjust system volume, change system sounds and manage audio devices?

A. 

B. 

C. 

D. 

40. Which of the following options of control panel will give access to change the theme, desktop background, sound effects and screen saver in Windows 7?

A. 

B. 

C. 

D. 

41. Which of the following options allows you to create different slide shows within the same presentation in MS-PowerPoint 2010?

A. 

B. 

C.

D. 

42. Which of the following statements is INCORRECT about URL (Uniform Resource Locator) name on internet?

A. It never contains spaces.

B. It always uses a forward slash (/).

C. It can start either with http:// or https://.

D. It must be written in uppercase.

43. Which of the following is an online storage service?

A.

B. avast

C.

D.

44. Which of the following statements hold(s) true about Control Panel icons in Windows 7?

Statement 1 :  is used to start using your voice to control your computer.

Statement 2 :  is used to change the sound scheme for your computer.

A. Only Statement 1
B. Only Statement 2
C. Both Statement 1 and Statement 2
D. Neither Statement 1 nor Statement 2

45. Select the CORRECT statement regarding Google Earth.

A. It represents 3D view of earth.
B. It is a translation service.
C. It is an operating system for wearables.
D. It is a video calling service.

ACHIEVERS SECTION

46. Which of the following is a free protection software provided by Microsoft for Windows 7 based computers to protect them from malware and spyware?

A. Personalization
B. Windows update
C. Windows Defender
D. Credential Manager

47. Aman has selected the data for creating a chart. Which of following shortcut keys creates a chart immediately but it might not be the best chart for the data in MS-Excel 2010?

A. Alt + F11
B. Alt + F1
C. Ctrl + F11
D. Ctrl + F1

48. A Slide Master view is used to change the design and layout of the master slides. Which of the following options of the Slide Master tab can be used to change the overall design for your slides in MS-PowerPoint 2010?

A. Placeholder
B. Themes
C. Setup
D. Align

49. Identify the following feature of MS-Excel 2010.

- It is used to create a link to a webpage, a picture or a program.
- It can be accessed by Ctrl + K keyboard shortcut.

A. 

B. 

C. 

D. 

50. Select the odd one out.

A.

B.

C.

D.

SPACE FOR ROUGH WORK

ANSWER KEYS

1.	(C)	**2.**	(D)	**3.**	(B)	**4.**	(B)	**5.**	(D)	**6.**	(B)	**7.**	(C)
8.	(B)	**9.**	(B)	**10.**	(A)	**11.**	(A)	**12.**	(B)	**13.**	(A)	**14.**	(B)
15.	(D)	**16.**	(B)	**17.**	(D)	**18.**	(B)	**19.**	(D)	**20.**	(B)	**21.**	(D)
22.	(A)	**23.**	(C)	**24.**	(A)	**25.**	(B)	**26.**	(C)	**27.**	(A)	**28.**	(B)
29.	(A)	**30.**	(A)	**31.**	(B)	**32.**	(A)	**33.**	(B)	**34.**	(C)	**35.**	(C)
36.	(A)	**37.**	(C)	**38.**	(B)	**39.**	(C)	**40.**	(A)	**41.**	(A)	**42.**	(D)
43.	(D)	**44.**	(C)	**45.**	(A)	**46.**	(C)	**47.**	(B)	**48.**	(B)	**49.**	(B)
50.	(D)												

SOF
SCIENCE OLYMPIAD FOUNDATION

National Office: Plot 99, First Floor, Sector 44 Institutional area, Gurugram -122 003 (HR) India
Email: info@sofworld.org | Website: www.sofworld.org
Regd. Office: 406, Taj Apt., Ring Road, New Delhi-110 029
Note: Please address all communication to the National Office only.